ORGANISATIONAL DESIGN

ORGANISATIONAL DESIGN

WHAT YOUR UNIVERSITY FORGOT TO TEACH YOU

ANDREW OLIVIER

Library of Congress Control Number: 2012913212

ISBN:	Hardcover	978-1-4771-4889-1
	Softcover	978-1-4771-4888-4
	Ebook	978-1-4771-4890-7

To order additional copies of this book, contact:
Xlibris Corporation
1-800-618-969
www.Xlibris.com.au
Orders@Xlibris.com.au
501877

CONTENTS

Background

What Every Leader Needs to Know About Designing Structure 9

SECTION I: THE SEVEN KEY PRINCIPLES

The Benefits of Using These Principles 17

The Sequence of Events: The Importance of Using a Process 19

The Principles 20

Principle 1: Business Intent and Required Complexity 20
Principle 2: Optimal Size 30
Principle 3: Making Decisions equals Work 51
Principle 4: Reporting Distance 59
Principle 5: Empowering Role Relationships 63
Principle 6: Matching Individual Capability to Role Complexity 86
Principle 7: Ensuring Leadership Coherence 89

Summary 92

SECTION II: THE SEVEN LEVELS OF WORK COMPLEXITY

A Closer Examination of the Vertical Dimension With Illustrative Stories.... 97
An Overview of the Work Domains38 97

Structure of Work Level Descriptions 104

Work Level I—Also Known as Quality 106

Work Level II—Also Known as Service 111
Case Study: Building a Private Military Corporation[39] 116

Work Level III—Also Known as Practice 118
Case Study Continued: Building a Private Military Corporation 123
Case Study: Building a Corporation 125

Work Level IV—Also Known as Strategic Development.................... 128
Case Study Continued: Building a Private Military Corporation 134
Case Study Continued: Building a Corporation 138

Work Level V—Also Known as Strategic Intent 140
Case Study Continued: Building a Private Military Corporation 148
Case Study Continued: Building a Corporation 150
Case Study: Building a Social Entrepreneurial Business 153

Work Level VI—Also Known as Corporate Citizenship 160
Case Study: Tesco...166
Case Study Continued: Building a Corporation 170
Case Study Continued: Building a Social Entrepreneurial Business........173

Work Level VII—Also Known as Corporate Prescience 175
Case Study Continued: Building a Corporation 178
Case Study Continued: Building a Social Entrepreneurial Business........183

Work Level VIII—Also Known as Corporate Sustainability 185

SECTION III: NEW CASE STUDIES

Case Study 1: Ericsson India. A Personal Reflection
on the Seven Principles of Design.. 191

Case Study 2: The Road Ahead: The Royal Automobile Association
(RAA) of South Australia (2007-2012) 198

Case Study 3: Integration of Two Latin American Mining Services Companies 218

Conclusion 233

Interested in Taking These Principles Further? 235

With Thanks 237

Notes and Bibliography 239

Index of Figures 247

Index of Tables 249

Index 251

Background

What Every Leader Needs to Know About Designing Structure

At some point in most managers' careers, they will be called upon to design organisational structure. As they attain positions of seniority, they will realise that competence in the design of structure and how it is populated makes the difference between success and failure. As the world connects and waves of change increase in rate and size, the need to adapt and change is now a constant for many organisations. The basic organisational principles outlined in this book, once in place, allow for adaptation and flexibility to occur more readily.

The fundamental principles outlined in this book are essential for all managerial leaders and practitioners. This book seeks to equip leaders with the seven key principles for creating healthy work systems through *effective structure* and *effective work* through *role design and role relationships*. The applications are highlighted throughout with case studies, examples, and work-based exercises.

This book is grounded in the thinking of Dr Elliott Jaques whose thinking may have been influenced and enriched by significant contributors such Herbert Simons, S. S. Stevens, John Isaac, Melanie Klein, Kurt Lewin, and those who worked with him at Brunel University in the early years, in particular Gillian Stamp. Over the years, many people and organisations around the world have added knowledge and evolved practices.

The concept of a *requisite organisation* (RO) is based primarily on the unique and integrative understanding of Dr Elliott Jaques[1] and Lord Wilfred Brown, who were the pathfinders and originators of these complexity-based models. Jaques pioneered a unique framework of leadership and an understanding of work. A prolific writer of books (some fifteen books on management) and articles, he was originally a medical practitioner, then a psychiatrist, and later a psychoanalyst.

He brought clarity of thought and a rational understanding to the very nature of what work is, how work should be structured to be felt fair, and how to create viable working relationships in an organisation. Effective role relationships were at the heart of his work. This plus his focus on the issue of time span of decision-making saw the emergence of quantitatively and qualitatively distinct levels of work or strata in any goal-directed human endeavour. Much of the development took place through experiential learning, either conducted by Jaques himself and/or through research carried out by many others as they implemented these ideas.

Jaques described his work as scientific management (an indication of its modernist genealogy), and he postulated various principles which are observable, measurable, and replicable Jaques first introduced his ideas in the 1940s and 1950s in the Glacier Project in the United Kingdom (Elliott 1951) while he worked as a consultant for the Tavistock Institute.

The Glacier Project was a major breakthrough in management and systems thinking and generated a great deal of academic debate (Gray 1976). However, criticism was levelled at the theories for being 'the truth' and damming it because it left no place for any other theories.

> 'Because it is a closed system of propositions, it—on the surface at least—appears to reject any alternate form of theory, giving it the superficial appearance of mutual exclusiveness. And anyone . . . knows that any theory not open to inclusion with existing theories is doomed to expulsion from the academic ranks.' (McCarty and Gray 1976, p. 10)[2]

How prophetic were these words! It is rare to find Jaques's models and theories taught in universities, and the only route to discovering his scientific principles of management is through consultants, reading his books (which are not for the faint hearted), or joining a discussion group or a not-for-profit organisation like Global Organisation Design Society.[3] This is unfortunate, as it has robbed generations of leaders of a set of rich models offering robust and coherent constructs.

Whether a supporter or detractor, it is the only coherent, complete system of scientific approach to leadership available, *and evidence would suggest that it works.* Karl Popper, the Austrian-born British philosopher, remarked, 'What was once thought can never be unthought.' Once a person really understands the nature of these principles and how to apply them, they realise that they possess a powerful lens to understand and design work, and *this can never be unthought.*

Brown, in his article 'The Legacy of Elliott Jaques' (2011)[4] says there are three camps—the believers, the non-believers, and the sceptics. There is however a fourth group, the biggest group by far and the most alarming—those leaders, academics, graduates, coaches, mentors, managers, and CEOs who don't even know it exists.

To underscore this point, a 2011 literature review entitled 'Leadership, Culture and Management Practices of High Performing Workplaces in Australia: The High Performing Workplaces Index[5] compiled by the University of New South Wales, The Australian National University, and Copenhagen Business School, and commissioned by the federal government's Department of Education, Employment and Workplace Relations, did not contain *a single reference* to Jaques and the practices of RO, although it has been practised in Australia for decades.

However, despite this, Jaques's body of work in different guises has been in constant use for fifty plus years in diverse organisational and business settings and across different cultures.

Jaques's models comprise three separate strands woven together into an overall model sometimes referred to as RO (as required by nature) or science-based leadership.

- People
- Structure and work
- Effective managerial practices

It is not the smokestack Taylor hierarchical view that its detractors like to use as a label. Neither is the rigid and static model of the organisational chart of the seventies, eighties, or even nineties. It is definitely not the fuzzy, seamless, leaderless structures suggested in interpretations of a networked organisation. It is about naturally occurring hierarchy, which has nothing to do with power or prestige but about managing the complexity of uncertainty and ambiguity. Tim Allan offers an annotated bibliography on hierarchy and a very useful short summary of Herbert Simon's 'The Architecture of Complexity.[6]

It is a story that, while continually evolving, offers a blueprint for understanding and organising the human enterprise based on *mutual trust and felt-fair relationships, which is supported by a robust set of principles that continue to be relevant because it is naturally effective.*

Some organisations have used the models, in full or in parts for four decades, surviving successive changes in leadership. There are now many well-documented case studies. For example, the US Army[7] has used the SST model (an earlier version of *levels of work*) extensively in the redesign of the US Army post Vietnam. Jaques was recognised by General Colin Powell for his work in restructuring the Joint Chiefs of Staff, the US Army, and the Surgeon General. The US Army Behavioural Institute has also done a great deal of analysis and research into SST and human capability, which only declassified was in the mid-nineties.[8] A full case study is available online at the Global Organisation Design Society complete with audio recordings, publications, and bibliography that document thirty-five years of RO development.

It was used in British Gas to assist restructuring before its privatisation and continues to be used by BHP Billiton, RTZ, and the Anglo American Corporation. It has also been used for more than seventeen years by Novus International.[9] Other users include Tesco (since 1995), Unilever, ICI, and the Anglican Church in the United Kingdom. It has a large following in Canada, where a number of organisations have used RO over the years and where Jaques taught and was based for many years.

In Argentina, Jaques built up a core following, and together, they worked with a number of companies that embraced the RO model. RO is still alive and well in Argentina and in a number of South American countries. A South American case study is in included in Section III. Some organisations (Acindar Steel, Argentinian Tax Office, Conarco, and Parona Metal SA) have seen RO embraced by their successive CEOs. In 2009, the Global Organisation Design Conference was held in Buenos Aires, and a number of companies presented papers on their work stretching from the seventies to the present.

In Australia, the RO and levels-of-work model has been used continuously with varying degrees of success. The CRA, the organisation where much of Jaques's work took place over an extended period, saw many Australian executives schooled in SST. Many of these executives, when they moved out of CRA, took the models with them to blue chip Australian organisations such as Telstra and the Commonwealth Bank and into a number of independent consultancies. The list is far too long to do justice, and this is not a literature review. The Royal Automobile Association of South Australia is an Australian case study included in Section III.

The principles for structure and role design appear valid across different cultures, nationalities, and different industries in paid and non-paid work and in the public and private sectors. They have found homes in culturally diverse settings that span Argentina, Australia, Belgium, Botswana, Brazil, Cameroon, Canada, China, France, Belgium, the Netherlands, the UK, Iraq, India, China, South Africa, Namibia, New Zealand, the USA, Uganda, Zimbabwe, Sweden, Singapore, and Norway. A useful collection of articles, interviews, and publications are available at the Global Organisation Design Society[10]

RO is not a luxury or a fad. It has proven worth with a strong track record. I hope this book will provide an entry point into this body of knowledge. Armed with this knowledge or even a portion thereof, we can build better organisations with greater responsibility and accountability, more humaneness, and a greater understanding for the importance and often fragility of the contexts within which they are embedded. Hopefully, these principles will help build healthier work places which are wiser and have a long-term focus.

It may also offer a route to sustainability by pushing out time spans of decision-making. A failure to think for a longer term and lift game plans will see many organisations join the ranks of extinction. The lifespan for a medium-to-large organisation is on average forty years at the present time. A policy of limitless growth cannot be supported any longer—we don't have the six more planets,[11] so we need to be thinking smarter about our company, long term.

Section II and III of this handbook present a number of case studies and observations to illustrate the seven key principles.

SECTION I

The Seven Key Principles

The Benefits of Using These Principles

- They are practical, well researched, and proven with the passage of time.
- It is the *only* system where *time* plays a key role, so it encourages forward thinking. Also, outcomes of each role can be measured and grouped according to passage of time to complete tasks. It is thus *outcome* focussed.
- It provides a common language about what to every leader *needs to know*, *to be*, and *to do* in order to run a high performance work system.
- It provides a common language to talk about *work* wherever the users may be.
- It clarifies role relationships and the requisite authority needed to make work decisions so as to avoid role relationship confusion, wasted time, money and resources.
- It is about building and holding trust through design which allows for the exercise of individual judgement and discretion. The seven principles establish a transparent felt-fair system with practices that reinforce strong working relationships which are aimed at achieving better business outcomes.
- It is a design blueprint. Provides the rigour for the design of resilient work systems through requiring the application and adherence to known and understood principles.
- Provides the rigour required for the analysis of work system and can highlight why areas are dysfunctional and how they can be improved.
- It offers a systematic way to decide who can take what job, depending on the complexity level.

- It enables a framework for individual development, organisational learning, and information architecture.
- It is a framework for understanding and liberating innovation and creativity at each work level, as well as the positioning and leadership of projects according to the degree of complexity required by the undertaking.

The Sequence of Events: The Importance of Using a Process

Using the seven principles requires discipline, and having a process to follow helps builds this rigour. Here is a suggested sequence of events for designing an organisation or to create a work team to achieve a specific intent.

The *sequence of events* is as follows:

1. *Where are we going?* Decide where we are going, and what is our intent and our purpose for organising.
2. *How are we going to get there?* Determine what strategies are the most effective to accomplish the intent.
3. *How will we organise ourselves?* Decide the required functions, structures, and roles needed to deliver on the strategy.
4. *What work needs to be done?* Decide what actual work needs to be done.
5. *How are roles related and what authority do they need to carry out their accountabilities?* Decide how to link and empower the work systems effectively.
6. *How do we recruit and deploy people effectively?* Deploy people who are in flow with the work challenges.
7. *How do we ensure effective leadership?* Ensure that Managerial Leadership competencies are taught for coherence and continuity.

Effective structure will be determined by the following principles of design which are organised in order of importance.

The Principles

Principle 1: Business Intent and Required Complexity

What degree of complexity (uncertainty and ambiguity) does the business intent generate? That is a guide to vertical structuring. How many work levels are needed to deliver the organisation's intent? There are a maximum of seven levels of work with each work level dealing with increasing work complexity and offering a unique value add which is essential in structural design.

What Is Meant by Work Complexity?

The first basic principle is that goal-directed human endeavour will emerge into a hierarchical structure of *effective* function and accountability. This is not a hierarchy based on power or privilege but one with different degrees of complexity.

The law of requisite variety states *that as external complexity increases, internal complexity must also increase if an organisation (or organism) is to handle the external environment effectively*. Failure to read our context and to be able to predict it spells extinction.

The different levels of work complexity emerge organically through entrepreneurial activity or may be introduced into an organisation through conscious design, either in response to a need or installed with intent in a Greenfield site.

Complexity may be defined in terms of the number of variables operating in a situation, the clarity and precision with which they can be identified, and their rate of change.

Behaving like a complex adaptive system, *each level does the best it can, getting on with what it is good at while nested within a sustaining and nourishing environment created for it by the work level above.*

The recent advances in the sciences, especially the biological sciences have helped enormously with our understanding of business as a dynamic complex adaptive system (CAS).

Complexity science and the CAS have helped to verify the validity of the seven principles. Fundamental to the complexity-based models is how complex adaptive systems, such as organisation change when reactng to new stimuli. Complex adaptive systems organise themselves spontaneously to cope with changes in their environments and thus prove extremely resilient and adaptable.

The Noble Prize winner Ilya Prigogine understood that a CAS will move to higher levels of complexity when the *energy moving into the system requires a higher form of processing ability*. If the rate of energy coming into the system is too great, the system has two responses—adaptation or implosion. It would seem that nature shuns equilibrium. Equilibrium or stasis would seem to precede extinction.

As the business environment becomes more complex, companies may add new levels of work and adapt to changing circumstances. Like ecosystems, they strive to maintain their resilience. Human enterprise. are continually trying to grow and lift their game plans and, in doing so, often move from one level of work complexity to a higher order.

Or they are trying to be more effective within their current work levels. Whatever the nature of the response, life strives for abundance—naturally rearranging its parts to cope with the situation more effectively and seeking to adjust within a band of tolerance in order to accommodate internal and external fluctuation and pressures.

It is the ability to adapt, to be flexible, and to change in order to cope with increased energy and complexity that allows a CAS to transmute to a new level of existence. This change can be spontaneous in evolving natural systems, and the most striking part of the equation is that the system is able to increase its own internal complexity in response to external influences.

This may be through the following:

Adding more parts.

- Repeating the use of irregular shapes for different purpose up and down the scale of complexity (levels of work have fractal patterns).
- Through more complex relations between the parts.
- Through more complex behaviour of the parts.
- Through assimilating new parts or creating new parts.
- The relationship between the system and its environment is non-linear.
- The system can be influenced by or can adapt itself to its environment.
- One may also get instances of the different systems coming together to form a larger whole that operates as a single system at a higher level.

Table 1 illustrates that there are, according to Jaques, seven work levels arranged in increasing complexity of decision-making. The work levels may be referred to as a numbered level (e.g. work level I) or by a work theme, denoting its work focus.

Each work level has a different unique value add, and none can be omitted if one seeks effective and healthy organisations. Missing work levels have negative impacts on performance, organisational health, and employee well-being. In the same way, not all organisations need to operate at level, but the number of levels in an organisation is related to their context, their objectives, and the complexity that needs to be engaged with in order to be viable.

An entrepreneur's view of 'where are we going' mostly evolves and changes with time and opportunity. However, a common denominator for success is getting work level I (Quality work) in place. This is the work level on which future success is built and appears to be an essential component for success. Work level I must work effectively to allow any other work levels to be added. The Law of Requisite Variety states that new work levels will emerge in response to increasing complexity and ambiguity in the organisation's operating environment or face collapse.

An example of this is the early days of growth of the Facebook, where the entrepreneur starts fiddling with an idea. It was not Mark Zuckerberg's only project, but he was obsessed with quality, simplicity, performance, and outage. While not having a clear business plan, he had a clear tactical strategy of what he was going and how to manage the process. In those early days of Thefacebook, he did have a strategy—a rare resource for an Internet start-up; that is, being able to pace its growth by only turning on new schools (universities) when they had the servers and resources to cope with the surge of usage. Once stabilised, they found resources to handle the next growth spurt.

He had a very definite view on the resources he needed but was not willing to comprise his values on advertising to obtain the resources, so they slowed the growth to match the resource availability. The twenty-year-old CEO was obsessed with quality—the theme of the first level of work, and for him, this was to ensure the system worked technically well with no performance disasters. Zuckerberg says, 'We didn't just go out and get a lot of investment and scale it. We kind of intentionally slowed it down in the beginning. We literally rolled it out school by school.' This allowed the first level of work to be laid well and provided the platform on which organisational complexity could be supported.

Initially, he and his group of mates did everything themselves—hard work aided by luck, and the serendipitous arrival of technologies like broadband (the early social networking were dependent on dial-up), and open source software which had just come of age to support such a venture. Zuckerberg was twenty, clearly holding a number of emergent work levels in his young brain, while ensuring the foundation building block was robust. The company's only real costs in those early days, even with 100,000 users were the servers and salaries. As Thefacebook grew, so it would add in new work levels, but first work level I—the quality stuff—had to operate iteratively and faultlessly. This it did and still does.

This pattern is common to all start-ups who get past first base. Consider another example of someone who makes chocolate. The entrepreneur does everything themselves initially. As she becomes more successful and the client base grows, she may start to employ others to assist her.

She may employ someone to do the accounts, another to answer the phones and emails, update the website, take orders, resolve queries, and do general work. Suddenly work level I is in place, and work is delegated. As her business environment becomes more complex, so the work levels start to emerge in response to the need to produce more and to distribute to new and more geographically remote outlets. Depending on the speed of business growth, she may decide to employ another person to help with production. She may outsource her accounting or employ a person to help with the books. Some software systems have to be installed to track orders and accounts, the website upgraded to process orders, and a login facility for suppliers and customers. Now work level II is in place, and she is now managing firmly in work level III.

Five years down the track 'where the company is going' may change. It may have been emerging in her mind as she dealt with the practicalities of running the business. Now the entrepreneur has moved up her game, letting go of personal involvement in work level I and II. She is now holding at least two work levels in mind as she deals with new emergent complexities of work level IIII and even some IV issues. Long-term planning includes an outsourced distribution network, new production premises, new-look retail outlets, and an expanded product line. This can only be done while ensuring that work level I—Quality—is still intact. If people don't like or want the product, that will mark the end of the business. Sustainability, ensuring low carbon footprints, and franchise requests are also part of her new workload. She can already see the need for an operations manager.

The point of this example is the need to have the requisite work levels to deliver on the strategy. The organisational intent determines the requisite number of levels for her enterprise, and this is a dynamic part of the equation.

Another example of *introduction into an organisation through conscious design, either in response to a need or installed with intent in a*

Greenfield site, is that of a well-established communications company with a respected brand that is bidding for mobile phone licences in a developing region. The company is registered on the stock exchange in its home country and also through a number of business subsidiaries. It has a range of innovative products, services, strategic alliances, and business divisions, employing some two thousand people directly.

The board and CEO embark on deliberate growth intent to create a multinational organisation and to establish their brand in new countries. They win five licences over a three-year period and set about building five new business units, each with its own intent and level of work. The work level is matched to the most complex task required by the new country CEO.

The purchase of these licences presents an organisational development challenge to the parent company as it has to lift its own game from a work level V entity to a work level VI, and it is now responsible for a range of subsidiaries operating at different work levels.

In Section II, we examine how Richard Branson, Muhammad Yunus, and Eeben Barlow built their organisations through the work levels over the course of their working journey. As these entrepreneurs' own cognitive capability to handle greater complexity increased with time, they grew their organisations. Virgin expanded every time Richard Branson transitioned to the cognitive capability associated with a new work level. Muhammad Yunus's mission continued to expand, and his influence grew each time. Each time he transitioned to the cognitive capability to work at a more complex work level, he made significant changes.

Each of these well-known public figures (as did others, such as Bill Gates, James Lovelock, Nelson Mandela, Ayaan Hirsi Ali) created the conditions for the growth of their organisations (or thought leadership) through consciously seeking new opportunities that demanded a quid pro quo organisational response to deal with the greater external complexity. It should be obvious that not all organisations are successful in this, and many fail in their attempt to move to a higher level of organisational complexity.

For Branson and Yunus, it would take decades for work level VII to emerge, and it only emerged because the questions 'where are we going' and 'how will we get there' were the dynamic equation they could continually reformulate. Yunus wanted to eradicate poverty, Zuckerberg wanted an open world, and Branson, for much of his journey, wanted to improve services for people and have fun in the process.

But like all systems and like the very definition of work, there are always limits to everything. We need to understand that economic growth has limits, even if it is an inconvenient truth, and we need to build and plan accordingly. When Branson moved into work level VII capability, he changed his focus to sustainability. Yunus has always been driven by seeing the complete eradication of poverty.

The first two questions in the sequence of events ('Where are we going?' and 'How are we going to get there?') provides the anchor to peg the work level required. The resultant strategy provides the blueprint as to how we need to organise ourselves in terms structure and functions.

Unique Value Add and Time Span

As work complexity increases, so does uncertainty and ambiguity in decision making. This is central to understanding the basis of levels of work.

Understanding where we are going and how we are going to get there is about making decisions in the light of that complexity. Decision taking is defined as 'the making of a decision with the commitment of resources in response to a demand or need.'[12]

Table 1 below shows that each work level adds value in a unique way, and this is summarised under the heading 'Generic Unique Value Add'. Each work level has a discrete and different time span, which is the measure of time it takes to complete the most complex task in the role. Time span is more fully covered under Principle 3.

The context within which any business operates is subject to unpredictability. Uncertainty is addressed by having the appropriate number of work levels in place. The general rule of thumb is the broader the context within which a business plays, the more complexity and hence uncertainty is present in decision-making.

Within a level of work structure *level-specific* communication and data flows are critically important. Each work level under requisite conditions is a self-organising system, possessing a rich mix of positive and negative feedbacks that create their own patterns, and pattern recognition is a key way of recognising, learning, and understanding.

A requisite structure enhances employees' ability to respond spontaneously to events guided by an overall sense of direction and purpose which are key attributes of self-organisation (Morgan 1993, McMillan 2000). However, work is about achieving outcomes in an accountable structure.

The seven principles for designing healthy organisations may be applied to any organisation, regardless of size, functional grouping, or process.

Table 1: **Levels of work complexity**[13, 14]

Organisational level and work theme	**Generic unique value adds**	**Time span of decision outcomes**
Level I (Quality)	*Accomplish direct tasks*/hands-on skills—supervise direct work	Three months
Level II (Service)	*Manage team doing direct work* or do specialist work—research and analysis of specific issues	One year
Level III (Practice)	*Direct a programme*/blending components to meet goals/constructing, connecting, and fine-tuning systems, making most of resources—tactical strategies for existing products and markets	Two years
Level IV (Strategic Development)	*Coordinate and resource multiple programmes*/integrating, modelling new futures, new services, products, positioning the organisation. Strategic planning within scope of level V (Strategic Intent).	Five years
Level V (Strategic Intent)	*Direct a unified system and set direction/ policy*/overview of organisational purpose in context and accountability for sustainability of a unified work system (both direction and viability).	Ten years

Level VI (Corporate Citizenship)	*Coordinate multiple systems in the global environment*/reading international contexts to support/alert level V strategic business units—coordinating multiple work systems globally.	Twenty years
Level VII (Corporate Prescience)	*Direct multiple unified systems in the global environment*/sustaining long-term viability, defining values, moulding contexts, directing multiple work systems globally.	Twenty years (not more than fifty years)
Level VIII * (Corporate Sustainability)	*Coordinate numerous emerging/established global systems*/building long-term resilience by rewiring existing unified systems and creating the new in order to meet changed contexts.	Fifty to hundred years

*Emergent

The Domains

The work levels can be grouped together into 'domains' in terms of their focus, activities, and outcomes. This concept of domains of work is based on the insights of Luc Hoebeke. See Figure 1 below.

The first three levels are concerned with 'doing'—which may mean producing, selling, or providing services effectively and that may include being faster, quicker, more sustainable, longer lasting, and better than our competitors. This is called the Value Added Domain. It is here where most companies operate and 95 per cent of adult human work takes place. Remember that each work level is about appropriate decision-making, and by ensuring clarity of work focus, value is added incrementally towards achieving clearly articulated and well-thought-out organisational purposes.

If the first domain of work is about asking the questions 'how', the next domain is about asking the question 'why?' or 'so what?' The next domain moves away from the concrete activities of work to those which are far more complex, often abstract and represent progress by degrees over longer periods of time. These are the executive levels of the organisation, and this is where continuity of operations is maintained while the organisation follows its strategic intent to a new desired future. This may include JVs, M&A, new products, markets, and new technologies. Here, uncertainty and ambiguity can be seen as key resources for the future.

Figure 1: **Domains and levels of work** [14, 38.]

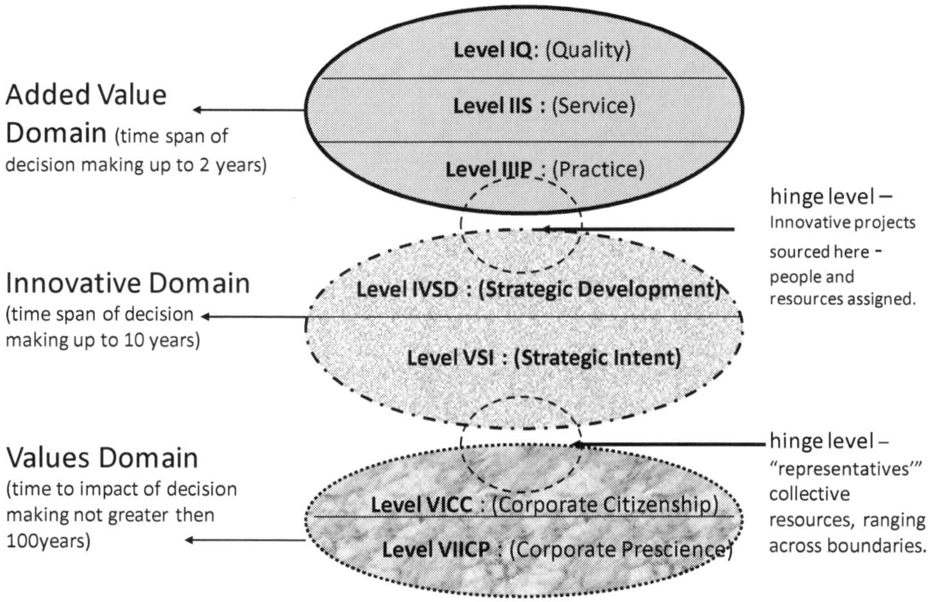

Acknowledgments ; Jaques, Stamp and Hoebeke. Adapted from the Working Journey©, Andrew Olivier 2012.

The third domain is that of multinational and international corporations and international bureaucracy. Here decisions are made on multinational and often global issues of resource allocation, integrated profit and loss statements and deciding where and in what to invest or disinvest and when and why.

This domain is concerned with integrated thinking across diverse fields of human endeavour within natural and human constructed whole system constraints.

This level of work is under increasing pressure as the policy of limitless economic growth starts to unravel while at the same time world demand for increasingly scarce resources continues to grow. Globalism has a come under scrutiny with modern technology able to bring the spotlight onto global accountability for fair work practices in developing regions.

Do you know?

- Do you know exactly how many levels of work there are currently in your organisation?
- Do you know how many you need?
- How would you find out how many you have?
- Do you have too many levels or too few?
- Do your Managerial Leaders spend the majority of their time on work appropriate to their level?

Principle 2: Optimal Size

The next question is, 'How will we organise ourselves?' This is more than how we group the organisation functions (e.g. production, operations, distribution, IS, HR, marketing) and addresses the underlying principles of design that should be applied for building scale while keeping a strong people relationship in all functions.

And with regard to ideal company size, yes there is a number . . . but it is not magic.

What is the optimal size for a company? Is there an ideal number of direct reports for a manager?

Author and physicist David Peat[15] talks about his conversations with David Bohm[16] (1917-1994) who was one of the foremost theoretical physicists of his generation. Bohm influenced among others, Peter Senge[17] and Joe Jaworski.[18] Jaworski is better known for his book *Synchronicity* his then ground-breaking work-in scenario planning for Royal Dutch Shell. Senge is well known for his ideas on a learning organisation.

Bohm said that when he worked with certain equations or numbers, it was as if they vibrated in his body, and they felt right. Bohm was a colleague of Einstein in the forty and fifties. Einstein's believed that as we are all part of the universe, made from the same building blocks, and certain properties such as numbers or profound ideas could cause resonance.

Bohm's own research led him to the view that there is an implicate order (Latin to be 'enfolded') which is a level of reality that lies behind the manifest—what he called the pre-manifest or precognitive. Simply put everything in the universe affects everything else because they are all part of the whole and physics at a subatomic particle level reinforces this.

This gives credit to the idea or sense that something just 'feels right' or 'something speaks to us'. We call this sometimes intuition or knowing. Peat also mentioned how Cezanne said the landscape spoke to him, urging him to paint.

Can We Apply This to an Organisation?

When one looks at organisational structures, there seems little consensus about what is 'right'. We find the most unwieldy structures with people floundering in a messy quagmire of unclear and foggy accountabilities and authorities and in large anonymous work groups or virtual teams where there is no personal relationship with their 'manager'.

Often this is compounded by a matrix-reporting structure filled with unaligned authorities, and where no one is actually accountable. Outcomes can vary hugely and often come at a high and unexpected cost. Organisational trust is often one of the first casualties.

Much depends on an organisation's structure. We need effective structures to deliver effective work but 'what feels right?'

Elliott Jaques's[19] *RO indicates that there is an optimal size and shape in designing structure. This is not arbitrary and lies on the application of a set of principle as a guide to action.*

Logically, most organisations start with the team. Almost all organisations start out this way—a group of committed individuals following a purpose. One can define a team as *a permanent or temporary group of people with a common purpose who must interact with each other in order to complete their tasks and for which they are held accountable.*

As the organisation grows, becoming more diverse and geographically spread the team remains the most fundamental grouping for getting work done.

The Mutual Knowledge Unit

The most basic building block in organisation life is the team. Organisational life will see a continuous stream of teams formed for this project or that purpose. Besides this ebb and flow, there are permanent teams within the formal organisational functions who are required to get on with the business as usual. While all teams qualify under this structural unit, we are specifically referring to the permanent grouping as the Mutual *Knowledge* Unit (MKU). Such a grouping is illustrated in Figure 2.

Permanent teams are normally comprised of team members and a team leader. In the more traditional sense, a MKU is seen as a work level I grouping of team members with a team leader (or in the more classic RO terminology, a work level II Front-Line Manager).

However, the MKU can exist between any two work levels where 'there is a closely shared business purpose and mutually complimentary roles reliant on delegated authority.' This may be any small unit—a start-up with an entrepreneur and a small team or a retail shop—for example, an outlet which is part of chain, a fashion outlet, a travel agency or a McDonald's restaurant. It may be a military unit such as a platoon or a CEO and his direct reports.

A MKU may also be a permanent cross-functional team who are involved in a work process and *who work together through a series of roles with defined authority and accountability but who may report to different managers outside the process*. This is dealt with more fully in Principle 5.

Principle 4 states that *one role must not report to another in the same level of work*. The rationale behind this is that for any managerial leadership system to be effective, a team leader *must function one level higher than his or her immediate reports*, and this makes it possible to exercise his or her vested authority without duplication, overlaps, or confusion.

By one level higher, we mean the role complexity is quantitatively and qualitatively different so that the Managerial Leader is able to offer the team member a different perspective on

- where are *we* going.
- how are *we* doing.
- what is *your* job.
- how *you* are doing.

And importantly, as the team leader, one must

- manage the team's decision-making process.
- issue tasks.
- allocate resources.
- set delivery dates and milestones.
- review and tend.
- assign and communicate authority and accountability.

Sound relationship management, essential for building trust, lies at the heart of the manager-employee relationship. Thus, having *a strong, trusting two-way, face-to-face working relationship aimed at achieving business objectives* is at the very base of the MKU.

Span of Control

Span of control is a concept created by an obscure Italian management consultant called A. V. Graicunas in the 1920s. No research seems to back this up and no ideal span of control has been advanced based on research. Increasing the span of control meant reducing the number of levels and was labeled organisational delayering so as to create more 'agile' organisations.

The current view on span of control indicates between 1-10 employees (median 7.8) per manager. Other research indicates 4-9 as being an optimal number because of the number of 'transaction channels' that is created every time a person is added to the team, while Wharton's research would indicate 5-12,[20] although acknowledging there are other factors than just the number of people in a team. Span of control is not a researched or validated concept and should not be a principle of design.

A work system needs to be structured with the right reporting distance (Principle 5), each role relationship with appropriately assigned authority to match the accountability (Principle 5) and *as long as Managerial Leadership competencies can be effectively carried out,* (Principle 7) than team size is optimal.

The Mutual Recognition Unit

MKUs exist within a larger context, and permanent teams exist within a function. So what is the basic building block of a work system comprised of multiple teams? A team gives us two work levels, each adding its values in different ways. When the organisation grows to a certain complexity level, a new level emerges. This three-level basic-building module in an organisation is the Mutual Recognition Unit (MRU) which has a level of work complexity added, namely work level III.

This now creates a three-tier structure. *Growth of the MRU can be organic*; for example, as an entrepreneur's business grows, he or she is faced at key points with resource decisions about employing others and delegating. This is a key transition point. For some entrepreneurs who do not have capability to operate successfully in this work level, the business fails in its growth bid.

Design can be a deliberate response to natural growth, product success, or a planned acquisition. The mobile phone company with its newly acquired licenses went through a process of deliberate design to create a number of organisations in each country with CEOs at the level of work required to deal with the complexity of the operations and strategy.

This new level of work does not refer to the old-fashioned disempowered rigid work hierarchy but an *emergent* hierarchy driven by finding solutions to manage the increased complexity required in its business environment. Biology, mathematics, and IT show us that hierarchy of function is part of natural design.

The MRU also allows a new organisational role to emerge in addition to the line-management roles of manager and supervisor, namely *the unique functions of the manager once removed (MoR)*. The three part nest of relationships is now;

MoR—> manager—> report once removed (RoR)

The key defining characteristic of the MRU is that the Managerial Leader must *know everyone in the work system*, and this happens not by accident or casual greetings. *It is through the functions of the MoR.*

The MoR must undertake three accountabilities in order to create the conditions for the levels below to flourish and to add their unique value:

- Build the talent pool and ensure succession planning is in place—answering the question, *what is my future* to RoRs. Remember the veto authority for appointments at the RoR level is shared with the manager.
- Ensure fair treatment and review of decisions where appropriate.
- Ensure consistency of leadership and its quality at the level below direct reports.The MoR is responsible for setting structure and role alignment.

The MRU concept 'feels right' as a design module. Consider the following examples.

Sir Richard Branson in his book *Business Stripped Bare*[21] says that in the early days, each time a Virgin company grew to a hundred people, he would split it and form a new company. The deputy MD and the deputy S&M manager became the heads of a new company, and this left him a pathway to promote and for empowerment. He reckons a business unit of a hundred is optimal *since it is personal and gives people clout*. Even today, he tries to keep the companies small and intimate.

James Lovelock,[22] the independent scientist who created the Gaia hypothesis about our planet, believes that the ideal human society size is a ship company ranging from 80-120.

Malcolm Gladwell who wrote *Tipping Point*[23] says the magic number is 150 since this number crops up all over the place and appears to be the requisite number for humans to work, relate, and be productive. He cites many examples.

WL Gore and Associates[24] is a company that manufactures high-tech fabrics in the US, and in 2009, it was voted fifteenth in the 'Fortune 100 best companies to work for' list. Seventy-three of those companies are still hiring, and WL Gore is known for its creativity and allowing employees to follow ideas. The late founder of the company said, 'We found again and again that things get clumsy at 150.'[25]

Prof. Muhammad Yunus,[26] the founder of the Grameen Bank and the microfinance industry, whose microcredit system has been replicated in developing areas around the world, said that when setting up a new branch of the Grameen Bank, they did it slowly and at a personal level. If you read the description of how Grameen started to function in a new area, the first rule was personal relationship building and creating loan circles that emulate the MRU in a different sense, 'When a branch receives the full repayment of the first one hundred loans and does so without the slightest hitch, only then can one feel satisfied that things are moving in the right direction.[27]

Figure 2: **Mutual Knowledge and Recognition Units**

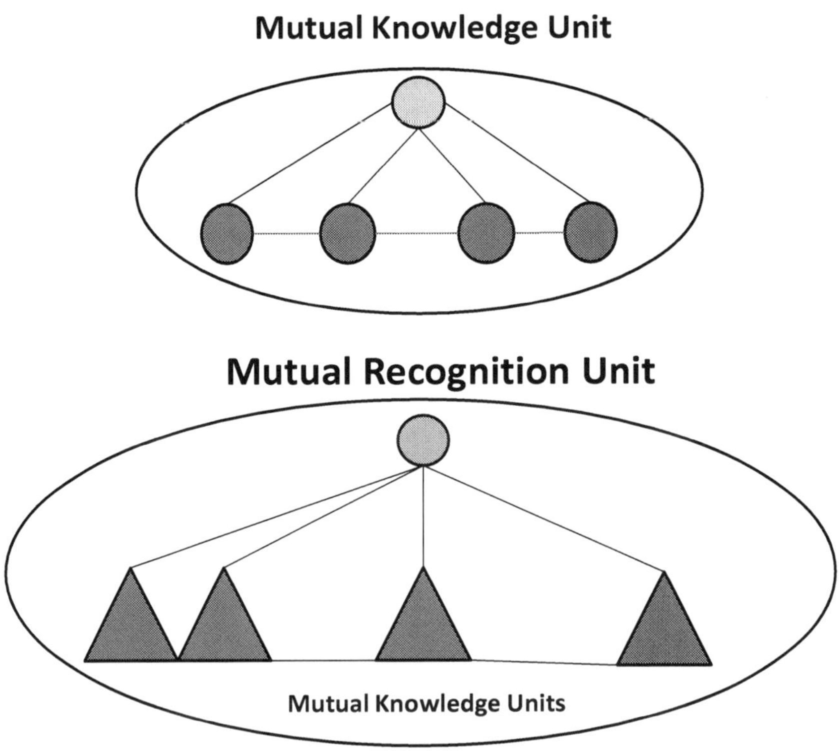

Yunus mentions that with setting up a branch, it can take up to two years before any structural problems become evident. In terms of the time span before outcomes can be determined, this corresponds with the MRU.

In the military, the MRU is the essential element of structure. The company makes up the social cohesive unit of an army and is composed of 120-150 people.

Bill Gates, when wresting with dramatic growth, felt 200 was the right business unit size as did a number of others, reported in *New Scientist*, which pegged 153 as the 'ideal size'.[28]

Levels-of-work analysis often uncovers extra non-value adding work levels (refer the RAA case study in Section III) and their removal. Integration or bundling achieves effective outcomes, with empowerment at each level, while still retaining the unique value adds and time span required for work-level differentiation. It also brings cost savings and productivity increases borne testimony by its longevity in companies that adopt the model.

The experience of Ricardo Semler[29] in restructuring Semco in the 1980s provides an example of discovering non-value adding layers and the gains that can be made from eliminating them. Semler identified that his organisation required five levels, and he restructured to create this many levels, each with clear unique value adds. The end result was an increase in clarity and organisational functioning as people's talents were 'freed-up' to be expressed.

Semler referred to how staff in the company *constantly complained that there were too many bosses and that they talked too much, and they were too slow to act*. He then describes how the need for promotion created many levels which led to . . . *But soon there is such a pollution of titles and levels—and a diffusion of responsibility and authority—that much of management's time is spent dealing with the inevitable conflicts, jealousies, and confusion*.

Figure 3 below illustrates what he did. He replaced the pyramid structure, which had multiple levels, with circles.

- The innermost circle would be himself and his own team, as he describes it, 'coordinating general policies and strategies'. He called these 'counsellors' (Work levels V and IV).
- A second circle enclosed the leaders of the business units, which he called, 'partners' (Work level III).
- And then the last circle, which holds everyone else, but within this circle would be

    ◦ Triangles—scattered around the outermost circle called 'coordinators'. As he says, 'These people would comprise the first crucial level of management . . . anyone who had a basic leadership role in our old system' (Front-Line Managers—level II).[30]

- Organisational delayering should only ever remove pseudo levels—removing a *real level of work will cause dysfunctional outcomes*, but it may take a while for that missing work level to emerge in poor performance, budget blowouts, or possibly damage to reputation and profit.

Figure 3: **SemCo Org chart design with work levels**

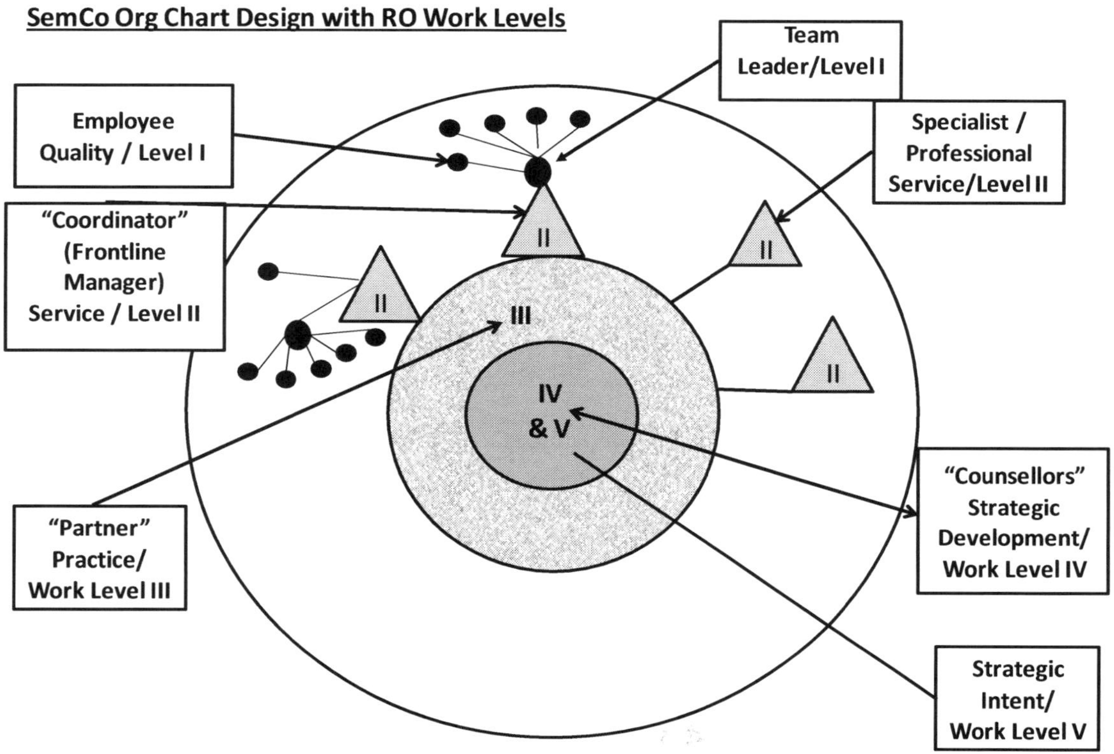

Acknowledgement Adam Thompson. Adapted and Used with Permission.

Another example of the importance of optimal size being determined by face-to-face relationships is the comment made by Craig Gisborne, one of the original members of Findhorn, a half-century young and well-established ecovillage based in the north of Scotland. He commented to me one evening, 'Our community used to be small, and we could all eat at the Community Centre. Now none of the community eat there. It's just the visitors and guests. Our size used to be ideal for many years—about 120, but now, our village has between 200 and 300 people living permanently here. I don't know their names, and I don't know what is happening in the community anymore. With all the visitors and the large community that live here, it's just too big. What will we grow into?'

After 300 people, the mutual recognition quality gets lost. Three hundred is the outer limit for any three-tier business unit or function size. Ideally the size of a MRU would appear to be between 100-250 for cohesion which generates a sense of place and 'belonging'.

An MRU can be a fully fledged business that is stand-alone where the entrepreneur or Managerial Leader is responsible for the business. In the former, it is about achieving sustainable growth and success or in the case of the latter, the effective delivery of known products and known services to a known client base.

The MRU can be chunked into functions for work level IV business units. Complexity builds on the organisation's foundation levels, doing what they do well, iteratively, over and over again. Only when that condition is met can another level of work complexity be added. The first three levels, the MRU, are about operational excellence, while the next two levels are concerned about positioning the organisation for competitive advantage and/or industry leadership.

Thus when designing structure, it is important to keep in mind the need for preserving the three-tier management structure (RoR—Manager—MoR) to ensure effective leadership and self-regulation which is aimed at working with and continuously improving delivery of known services and products to a known market in the most cost-effective manner.

Effective organisational architecture is a key element in allowing an enterprise to liberate its human capital. It is also the only effective way to proactively manage the uncertainty and unpredictability that exists at all work levels within an enterprise. Effective structure needs to allow for stability and effective processes, while at the same time providing freedom of entrepreneurship and innovation and for managerial leaders to really work with and know their people.

Another way of saying this is—*the architecture of a company reflects how it has attempted to limit uncertainty in its operations and, at the same time, how it has embraced uncertainty as a resource for its sustainability.*

This is done through following the principles—*getting the levels required for the strategy, ensuring role relationships are authorised, accountabilities shared and agreed and that the enterprise is built to a human-scale.*

Work will be organised in different ways. This can be around functions—with specific divisions/departments, by product (base metals, consulting versus auditing), by geography, by market segment, by customer size, or by a mixture of all. Whatever the choice for organisation, these principles need to be applied for effective design.

The three-tier block ensures a basic structure to create the optimal conditions necessary for each part to function and the ground work for feedback and system control. In larger organisations where the complement for work level III managers may number 300 or more, face-to-face knowledge is not always possible for the MoR at work level V. However, every attempt should be made by the level V MoR to know managers, and this should be undertaken through reviewing personal appraisals, CEO forums, workshops, gatherings, reward and recognition ceremonies, and company level induction.

The MRU is the basic module, or, in some cases, the complete company, and coherence comes through integrity and the quality of this particular form of managerial leadership.

Scaling Up

A Level IV led Business—a Business Unit, Division, or Function with a Number of Departments

- Time span of CEO/GM is between three and five years.
- Basic team-building blocks of MKUs present.
- Three-level structure of the MRU-present work levels I-III.
- MoR role present for work levels IV/II and III/I.
- Found within one geographical location.
- Well established and mature market(s).
- One or more established products/services offered to these markets.
- Number of functional departments that are codependent.
- Focus on quality, safety, and cost reduction/control/efficiency, best practices, and value control.
- Focus on delivering laid-down business objectives (from strategic intent at work level V[1]).
- Size may be up to 2,000 employees.
- May have one or more innovative projects with time span of delivery greater than two years. (Refer to Figure 4.)

1 If a standalone business - the Entrepreneur / CEO may hold work level IV and V together, as the business grows Level V may or may not emerge through organic growth or acquisition/merger

Figure 4: **A level IV led business**

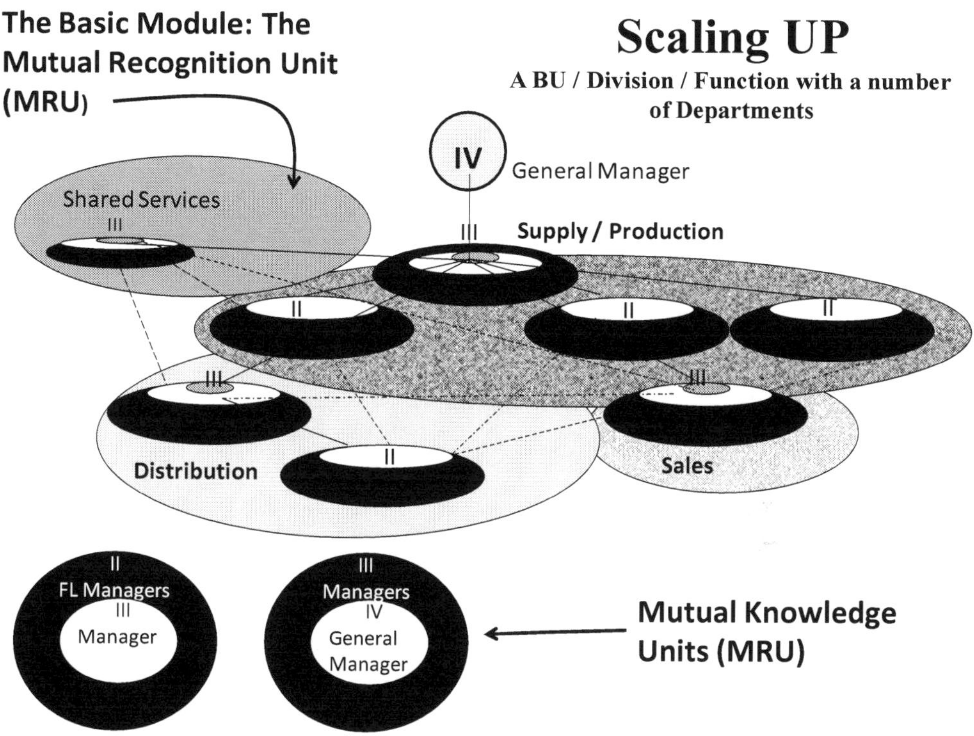

A Level V led Independent Business or Division Within a Group

- Time span of CEO and board is between five and ten years.
- Basic team-building blocks of MKUs present.
- Three-level structure of the MRU-present work level I-III.
- Executive leadership team of work levels IV and V (MKU).
- MoR role present for work levels V/III, IV/II, and III/I.
- One *or more* geographical locations—national (possible multinational).
- Range of brands; trademarks; well-established, mature market(s); industry player; and research and development possible.
- Image and reputation key factors.
- Multiple products/services/markets.
- One or more business entities at lower work levels.
- Number of functional departments, corporate services, and shared services.

- Focus on quality, safety, cost reduction/control/efficiency, and best practices.
- Focus on strategic intent—value control and value creation.
- Continually exploring growth and value creation opportunities through mergers, acquisitions, and joint ventures (new markets, new products, and new alliances).
- Size may range from 1,000-10,000 employees. (Refer to Figure 5 below.)

Figure 5: **A level V led business**

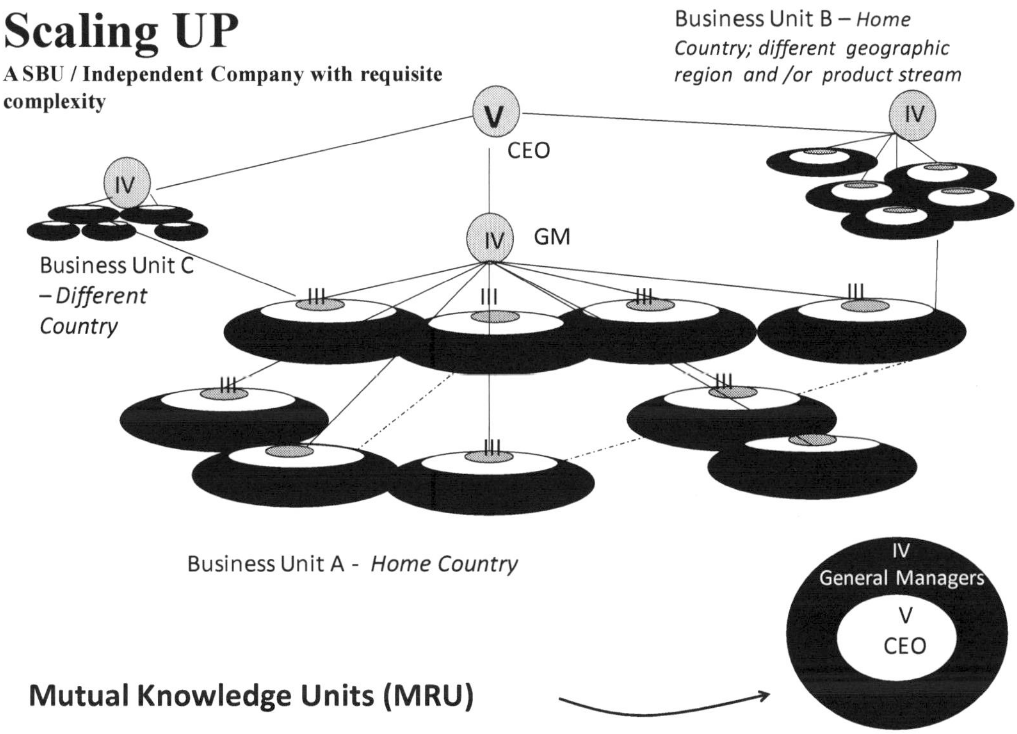

A Work Level VI Led Global Company

- Impact of decisions of group CEO, executive team and board—ten years plus.
- Maximum time span of operating entities and CEOs—five to ten years.

- Basic team-building blocks of MKUs present at work levels I/II, II/III, III/IV, IV/V, and V/VI.
- Three-level structure of the MRU-present work levels I-III.
- Group executive leadership team of work level V and CEO at VI.
- MoR role present for work levels VI/IV, IV/II, and III/I.
- Multinational, regional, and global presence possible.
- Range of brands; trademarks; well-established, mature market(s) and emerging markets.
- Key industry player, collaborative, influence on politics, economics, environment, and technology.
- Image and reputation key factors.
- Multiple products/services/markets/innovation.
- Well-developed research and development function.
- Multiple profit and losses—one or more work level V entities.
- Number of functional departments and corporate or shared services.
- Diversity of organisational structures to suit contexts within which it is embedded.
- Focus on quality, safety, cost reduction/control/efficiency, best practices, value control, wealth creation, and building of goodwill (strategic development).
- Size may range from 8,000-50,000 employees.

A Work Level VII Led Global Company

- Impact of decisions of group CEO, executive team, and board—ten years plus but not more than fifty years.
- Maximum time span of operating entities and CEOs—five to ten years.
- Basic team building blocks of MKUs.
- Corporate collegiate at VI and VII (MKU).
- Three-level structure of the MRU-present work levels I-III.
- Group executive comprised of work level V, VI, and CEO at VII.
- MoR role present for work levels VII/V, VI/IV, V/III, IV/II, and III/I.
- International network of owned entities—some full level V entities which are listed, range of brands; trademarks; well-established, multiple mature market(s), multiple industry player, collaborative (a network of entities).
- Influence on global stage of economics, politics, social, and environment. image and reputation key factors for network of

entities with corporate social responsibility well developed through trusts and foundations.

- Multiple products, services, markets, innovation, research and development, and new and emerging markets.
- Concern is viability of product range and R&D investment in the next generation.
- Investments in long-term options for twenty years plus.
- Multiple balance sheets.
- Number of products streams, corporate and shared services, complex value chains, and global logistical networks.
- Focus on quality and cost reduction, cost control, practice and cost efficiency, value control, and strategic development, strategic intent and value creation, corporate citizenship, and shaping of values.
- Size may range from 50,000-250,000 plus employees. (Refer to Figure 6 below.)

Figure 6: **A level VII led business**

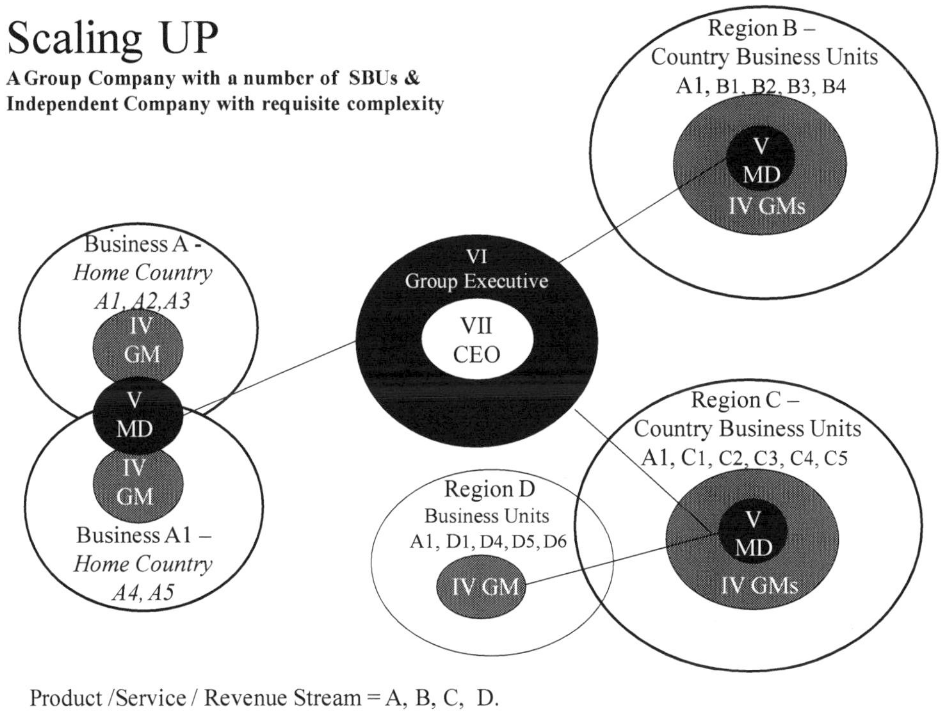

A case study of a deliberate strategy of building requisite-structured business units was undertaken by the telecommunications company MTN over the years 2001-2005.[31] The year 1994 not only saw the birth of democracy in South Africa but also the introduction of a new technology which was to become integral in communication and the tool of the new global village—the mobile phone. Mobile Telephone Networks (MTN) was founded in the fledgling democracy and expanded along with the innovations and developments in technology and products. This growth saw the company move from South Africa to include a collective of licenses in countries scattered across Africa.

Ten years later, in 2004, the company's vision was to be the leader in telecommunications in developing markets and as such went through a significant restructure to prepare for growth. Principle 6 states that one needs to 'match individual capability to role complexity', that is, ensuring people are well matched to deal with complexity in work. Part of the HR strategy in the first decade was precisely this—mapping individuals to positions and to focus on career development aligned to business needs.

The growth in the initial decade was understood in terms of Jaques's complexity and the shift in decisions in the most senior positions, and therefore, the increase in accountability and nature of the various roles was also understood.

As the company established itself, the focus of the work was strongly focused on establishing an effective operation with good coverage and products (the first three work levels) as well as creating the business models and innovations which adapted to and, at times, lead the market, for example, prepaid (a strategic innovation at Work Level IV which spread globally).

As the markets opened and the technology grew, MTN found itself operating in a number of countries with a range of political and legal environments as well as influencing diverse societies and cultures (South Africa, Uganda, Swaziland, Rwanda, Cameroon, and Nigeria), and managing and leading the array of business units needed a different structure and leadership. The company then embarked on a bold purpose of exponential growth in developing markets with all the challenge that it entails. This is illustrated in Figure 7.

Figure 7: **MTN organic growth**

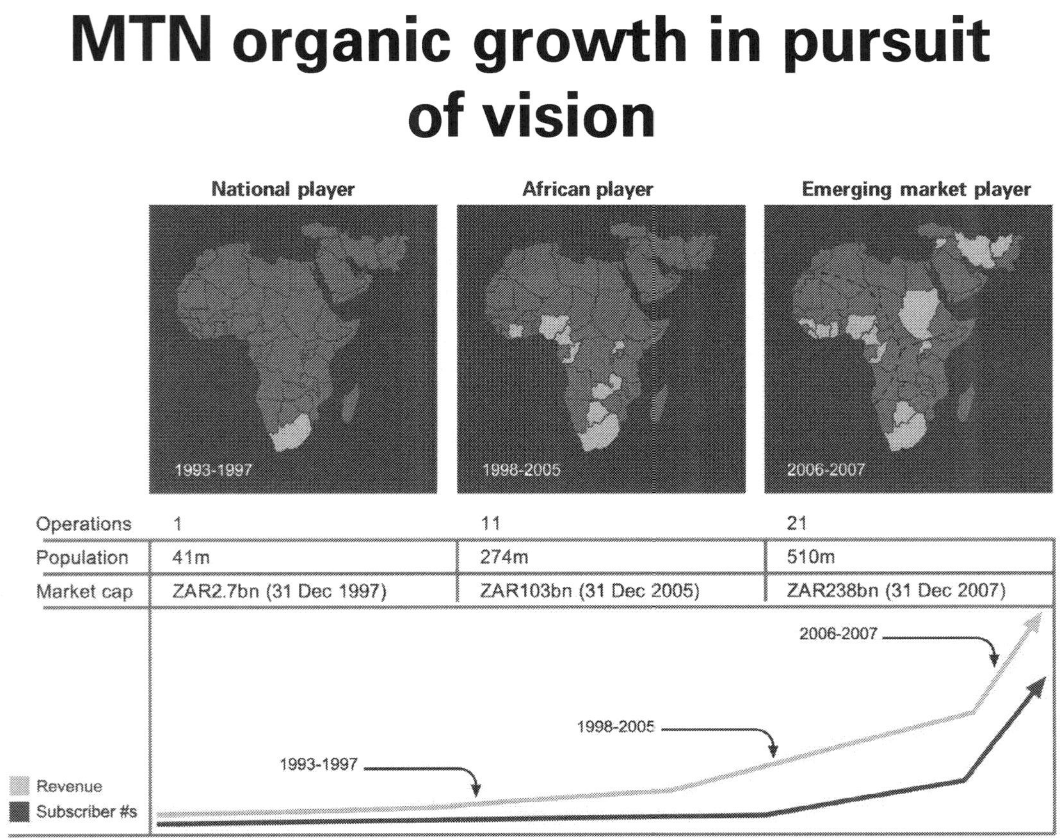

The construct of levels of work was used to categorise current business units and understand the scale and scope of the envisaged growth. For example, to lead and manage a relatively large organisation in an unstable environment with competitors, volatility, shifting legal and regulatory environments, and diverse cultures required a different type of work (and capability) than a smaller more operationally focused unit with fewer stakeholders. Table 2 shows that categories A, B, and C were created in terms of increasing complexity and different nature of work.

Table 2: **Characteristics of the structure templates**

Characteristic	Category A	Category B	Category C
Potential subscriber base	>5 million subscribers with potential to exceed 7 million	>1 million with potential to exceed 1.5 m up to 5 m	<1 million with potential to exceed 1.2 m
Level of Work Theme	Strategic intent	Strategic Development	High Practice to Strategic Development
Degree of autonomy—risk	High risk	Relatively high	Relatively high to medium
Talent requirements	High degree of specialisation	Broad-based specialists	High degree of generalists

Regions (e.g. Middle East and North Africa) would likewise include one large business unit (category A) and a spread of category B and category C operations. The management of the regions would be established at a level above the most complex of CEOs level of work. A central core was created to provide leadership as well as create the consistency in values, language, brand, culture, models, and process across the group.

With this model, MTN was able to grow from operating in a collective of six countries to an aligned strong, trusted brand, contributing to the societies and economies of twenty-one nations across the African continent and into the Middle East. The talent strategy and succession was aligned to the complexity of the different units as well as the future demands impacting the organisational development across the group. The application of the model was managed by the core but implemented consistently across all operations from Cyprus to Uganda to South Africa, becoming embedded in the culture and processes of the group.

In conclusion to this principle, a quick refresher of 'the sequence of events' is as follows:

1. Where are we going? *Decide where we are going—what is our intent and our purpose for organising.*
2. How are we going to get there? *Determine what strategies or strategy is the most effective to accomplish the intent.*
3. How will we organise ourselves? *Decide the required functions, structures, and roles needed to deliver on the strategy.*
4. What work needs to be done? *Decide what actual work needs to be done.*
5. How are roles related, and what authority do they need to carry out their accountabilities? *Decide how to link and empowering the work systems effectively.*
6. How do we recruit and deploy people effectively? *Deploy people who are inflow with the work challenges.*
7. How do we ensure effective leadership? *Ensure that Managerial Leadership competencies are taught to ensure coherence and continuity.*

Deciding what work needs to be done is the either benchmarking the required level of work (start point and end point) for each function in a Greenfield site or a review of each existing function in terms of where each part should be adding value.

This type of analysis is done through studying the strategies (and time spans), leading each function *as determined* by the CEO's mandate and which flows from point 1 in the sequence of events. Point 1 leads to 2 and so on. It is the strategies required which informs us about the requisite levels of work needed to achieve this. Point 4 focuses the mind on the main functions needed to do this and the levels of work required in each function.

Principle 3: Making Decisions equals Work

Principle 1 provides a vertical structure linked to the complexity of the undertaking, while Principle 2 provides a blueprint for building scale and keeping the people focussed.

Principle 3 requires clarity around what specific work needs to be done to achieve the intent. To ensure accuracy in determining work levels and required roles, one needs to analyse and identify the major work tasks required. The tasks arise from the intent and its associated strategy.

Work is accomplished through creating roles and grouping sets of essential tasks within each role. Such roles are encapsulated in a document referred to as a position description (PD).

PDs are a description of a dynamic but routine set of work expectations. Too often they are seen as static irrelevant documents. That is because the world of work is dynamic, and new tasks are continually emerging. PDs are an authorised system of work and are the way the CEO and board exercise managerial authority and accountability of a complex adaptive work system.

A System of Work

Defining the required work levels, functions, size, and PDs is part of the systematic description and documentation of work within the organisation. The CEO, and every manager, is accountable for this because they are authorised by the board to organise the work required to achieve the strategic intent.

A *system of work* is defined as 'a framework for a replicable set of events which are agreed to be necessary to achieve a specific and known purpose or set of purposes.'

So what are the minimum requirements for the effective documentation of work?

Everyone intuitively feels that running a large company is more complex than leading a team of production engineers. Wouldn't it be great to be able to measure the complexity of work in an organisation (and even assess who is able to handle what level of work) so as to get the number of levels correct to deliver on the strategy?

Time span is seen as a quantitative guide to the level of work complexity of any role at any level, while the unique value add is another mutually acceptable and complementary way of measuring the work level.

How Time Span Is Measured

. . . the time to completion of the most complex task in a role. This may also be described as the time that elapses before the Managerial Leader or team leader at the level above can see the completion of that task.

While it takes a few years to build a bridge or transform a large sales force to a new way of selling, it only takes a few months for a real estate to sell a house or half an hour for a dentist to fill a cavity in a tooth.

This common-sense approach underlies the concepts of work levels. Time span is not about trying to envision the future, which is a different issue and which is referred to as *time horizon*. Time horizon is relevant when we speak of individuals and their own individual capability to make decisions. For example, Facebook's CEO Mark Zuckerberg, as a twenty-year-old, had a vision of his company as 'a utility'—something everyone needed like water, power, and food, and his objective was 'to make the world a more open place'. He also said, 'The companies that have succeeded and have the best impact are able to outcompete everyone else are the ones that have the longest time horizon'[32] His early long-term decisions was not to compromise on advertising revenue and in holding a belief that was not about commercial gain.

The basic premise is that the longer the time span, the more complex the work and the more vulnerable the organisation to the quality of that decision-making. Jaques's research indicated that there is a systematic structure that was linked with target-completion times and which consistently revealed clear time cut-offs.

All businesses work with time, and it is in work levels I-V where time span is most relevant and practically useful. For example, work level II works with annual budgets while in work level III, managerial leaders are accountable for contributing to the next year's budget and plan. Work level IV and V need to be working on longer-term strategy with the organisation being guided by scenarios or broad statements of intent to guide decision-making at work level V. This could well be up to a ten-year period.

Thus for organisations operating up to and including work level V, a primary function of the board is to determine the time span of decision-making for its CEO and for the CEO, that of his or her direct reports and so on . . .

This means what by when and how it will be measured. Boards are accountable for viability of the organisation, and this starts with ensuring that the CEO is operating at the appropriate work level to deliver the most complex intent. *For line managers and their support, it is important when tasking to consider how long it will take before the task is completed and how does the role add value?* This basic question should be asked for each PD and by all project managers about project work (see Figure 8).

Figure 8: **The levels of work model showing unique value add and time span**

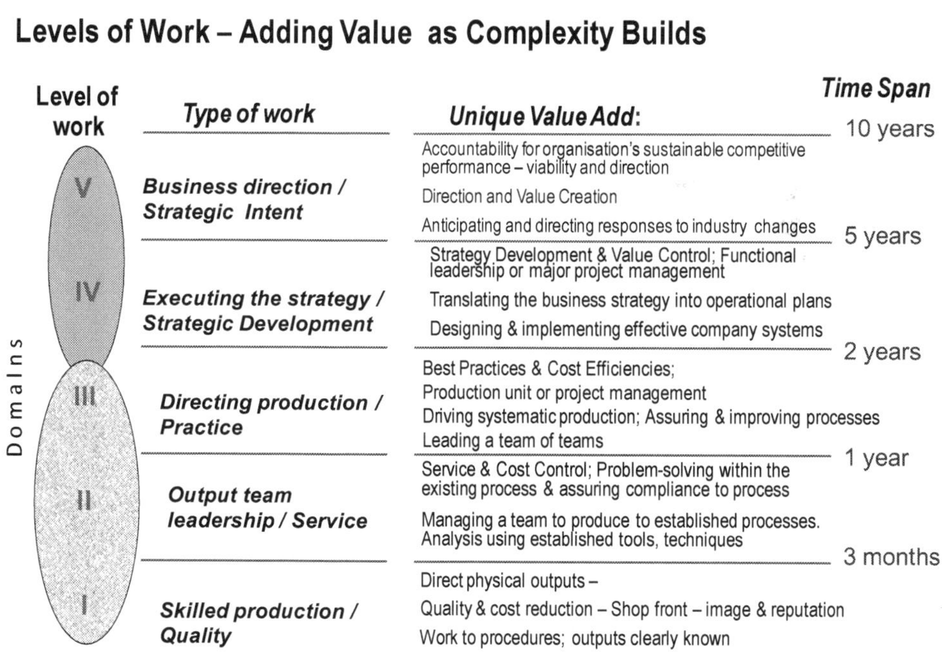

In practice, it would seem that time spans work well for operational roles but become less reliable and more difficult to ascertain (and less helpful to incumbents) for work levels VI and above when the ten-year threshold is crossed. With the rate of change increasing, some argue that time spans at the higher levels belong to an age of certainty now gone, and the best a CEO can do is hope to build resilience. Whether this assumption is valid or not, companies need to think ahead. Time spans of decision-making of major Australian companies in 2012 would seem to be in the order of five to ten years at maximum. Forget issues of climate change and limits of growth if those threats are too insidious for pragmatic boards and CEOs, consider future-focused work—survival. A full one-third of companies listed in the 1970 Fortune 500 had vanished by 1983. They had been broken up, sold, or integrated.

A more suitable measure for work levels VI and VII is *time to impact of decision—the amount of elapsed time before the outcome of the most complex decision can be confirmed.* At the ten-year mark, outcomes are more difficult to determine in advance, and one becomes alert to opinions, views, data, and signals to confirm the exercise of sound judgement. From a risk management perspective, such a measure encourages longer time thinking and might be applied to other work levels from a sustainability perspective.

Consider, for example, for the CEO of a level V organisation, the acquisition of a level IV company may only be regarded as having been a good investment some five years after the purchase, discounting short-term cost-saving synergies. This will be judged by the actual cost of integration, whether the promises of synergy were delivered upon through the creation of wealth for shareholders, community, customers, image and reputation, market position, and company share price. However, the actual task of acquisition and integration is three years. Both measures will classify this as a work level V task, but the impacts are increasingly important, especially if the purchase turns out to an asset that needs to be divested because it was a poor strategic decision.

Organisational Function (Design and Review)

Through the process of analysing UVA and time span of work, one can map out the required levels of work for the different functions within an organisation. Not all functions require the same levels of work. The determining factor will be the strategic intent of the CEO agreed with his or her board. This benchmark allows for pegging work levels of the executive team.

Figure 9 is an abbreviated example of such an output done at a leading Australian Bank. In our earlier discussion of the telecommunication company who were expanding with multiple new licences that had been granted in different countries, a similar exercise was undertaken, but specific organisational functions were replaced by the CEO's mandate for each country.

Figure 9: **Example of a function review**

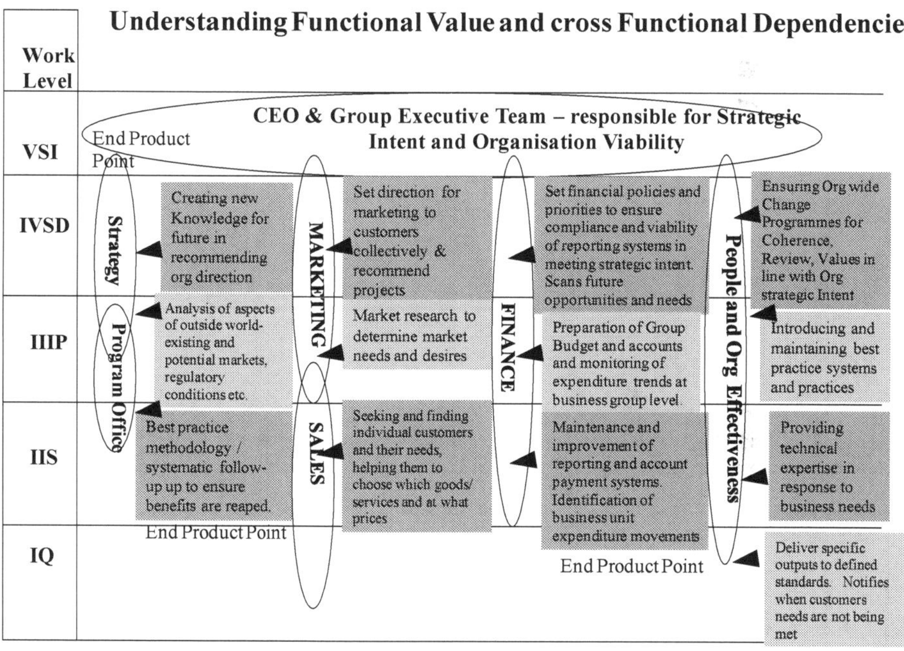

Acknowledgment to Les Hayley

Position Descriptions

PDs represent 'a system of work that documents and authorises the accountability of work required to achieve its strategic intent.' A PD may encompass the work of one or more people *who fulfil multiple roles.*

Roles may shift as needs arise. An effective PD must include the following fundamentals.

The purpose of the PDs existence—It is a summary statement which if designed correctly, should make explicit its unique value add (UVA). Each work level has a defined problem complexity, which is unique to it, and should create a unique value-adding proposition.

This defined problem complexity is similar across the spectrum of work within a work level. How long it takes to complete the most complex task is the key question.

Key Result Areas

This must cover the agreed work (normal) that needs to be performed. The KRAs are laid down in the documentation of the organisation's work. It cannot be arbitrarily changed.

A well-constructed PD will offer a set of key result areas or key performance indicators which will indicate the time span required to complete the most complex task and a description of how the outcomes are measured. If you are reviewing previously written PDs, it may require some investigation to work out time spans, but when the overall purpose of the PD is understood, this often becomes clear.

KRA set out the areas where the organisation requires outcomes. KRAs should link to a performance management system and should have key performance indicators (KRIs) stating performance requirements.

The PD should clearly state the role type plus its authority and accountability.

A PD may describe an individual who performs more than one role; for example, a PD may be for an operations manager who manages a full-time standing team and is thus a line-management role. It may also be a specialist role providing service to others, and thirdly, it may have a role as a team member on a project. Each of these role types should be clearly identified and the appropriate authority *and* accountability of each listed. This is discussed fully under Principle 5.

Examples of Poorly Defined Roles in an Organisation

When work is not clearly defined and Managerial Leaders do not set context and integrate new developments with existing work streams, you can get comments like this arising.

'I can see some of the things that come from strategy are flawed. It has not been clearly thought through, and I can see they won't work. The current structure makes you very reactive and reacting to issues created by the strategy. You are held accountable for things you knew that would not work and in which you had no say.

There are too many people creating strategy who have not had to deliver or even worse are not held accountable for that strategy. Strategy is not linked to implementation and seeing the results of what they have done.

It is an upside-down pyramid with no accountability. We have too many offerings and products, and I am trying to link them together with the unwilling and the unbelieving!

It also takes time to get anything done here, so bureaucratic, so many signoffs, and too many decision-makers, who quite frankly, don't seem to add any value as far as I can see . . .'[33]

A Tip

When adding or changing PDs within a work system, such as creating a new PD or removing an obsolete PD or modifying an existing role, never do it in isolation. Always consider the sequence of events and ask, 'What impact will my proposed changes have across the work system?'

Writing PDs should not be left up to HR. The Managerial Leader is accountable for the PDs of his or her Mutual Knowledge Unit (MKU) or Mutual Recognition Unit (MRU). They need to consider how changes are integrated, and how authority and accountabilities must be realigned. These recommendations are then approved by the MoR after checking alignment and structural integrity and that there is processes alignment and it has been integrated within their system of work. Remember, PDs authorise the systems of work of the company. Who and how they are changed cannot be random events.

Principle 5 looks at empowering role relationships through agreeing the authorites and ensuring understanding among stakeholders.

In assessing the level of work of a role, it will always be accorded to that of the most complex task.

Figure 10 shows a range of different tasks being undertaken across work levels I-IV. This is not a well-designed role, but there is one task that has a time span of more than two years *which makes it a low level IV role*.

Figure 10: **The level of work of a role**

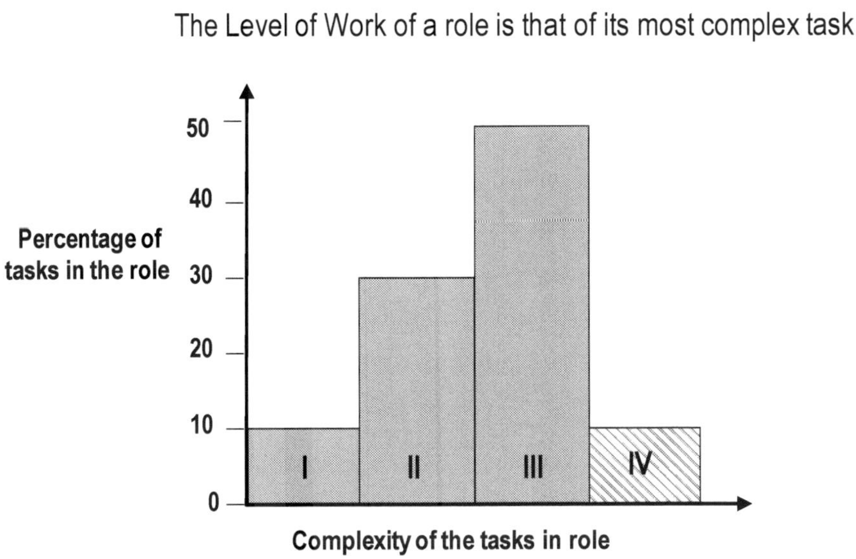

A work level can be divided into the following sub divisions:

- Low—A role which has less than a third of its tasks within one work level will make it a low work-level role.
- Mid—A role which has less than two thirds of its tasks within one level will make it a mid work-level role.

- High—A role which has more than two thirds of its work taking place in work level is a high work-level role.

A role which has a unique value add (UVA) described as work level III must be a work level III role. For example, if Figure 10 was such a role, the work level IV element must be removed. UVA = level of work of role.

A role which has a unique value add that is in work level III must have a task that has a time span appropriate to that work level.

UVA + time span = level of work.

A Note

Time frames may be subject to inflationary claims when people realise this is a measure. In a project work, budgetary milestones may help, but always check with the MoR. Some practitioners prefer to work with the balance of task accountability. In such a case, the level of work is the average of the sum total of the time spans involved in a role.

Principle 4: Reporting Distance

This principle is concerned with creating the right distance in the vertical structure. The rule is not to create overlaps and duplications, and the principle requires that one role must not report to another in the same level of work for some very sound reasons.

This is all too easy to happen with pay creep, business growth, apparent work overload, span of control, topsy role titles, hastily created structures, and personality-catered roles to mention just a few causes.

This is a common, costly, and creeping error in company growth, and lack of knowledge is the greatest cause. It can have devastating effects when occurring at senior leadership levels such as when the CEO leads the company into a new work level.

There are different types of reporting structures—the official organisational chart (the manifest structure), the way it actually works (the extant), and then there is the requisite structure (how it should to be).

In Figure 11, the design of roles A, B, and C are all negatively value adding to the purpose of the work system. They are poorly designed and the role relationships are unclear.

Figure 11: **What are we looking at structurally?**

A is a role stretched across multiple work levels which means that its unique value add will be confused or unclear. It is likely that the role authority will not match its accountabilities, and it will be trying to deliver too much to too many. It will disempower direct reports, and this effect will in turn disempower the work levels below that.

Bottlenecks, hasty, or inappropriate decisions and often changing priorities will characterise such a role, and the incumbent will be stressed and out of flow. The role should not exist and needs to be restructured or discontinued.

An example of this is the sales and marketing manager who is not comfortable with the level of work complexity of his role (Principle

6) and drops down to work at a lower level, thus getting in the ways of his direct reports. There are now confused unique value adds (Principles 1 and 3). The marketing manager is not leading the function at the appropriate level but is responding to competitor's campaigns—trying to beat them on price and service promises and issuing conflicting and confusing specials and starting price wars, hence damaging brand and losing market share over time. He has stepped into the unique value adds and authorities of his direct supports and disempowered them in turn.

B is a compressed work system with too many roles crowding each other. It is over managed with pseudo work levels. The unique value add of each role will be unclear with overlap and duplications. Authority and accountabilities will likely be blurred and fuzzy, yet everyone is really busy. Budgets will often be overrun, internal politics will be intense, there could be heavy overtime, and who is accountable for what may be an issue as well as who is reporting to who about what. The work system needs to be restructured and overlap or duplication removed.

An example is of the poorly designed call centre that has evolved over time, with many roles reporting to each other in the same work level but no one having clear authority to make a decision, so call centre consultants can shop around to get a decision they like.

C is a work system which is missing a level of work. This is manifested in a lack of traction in getting action on strategies or plans. Team members will have no immediate manager, so objectives may be unclear as there is no context and littler prioritisation. Resources are insufficient or unavailable, and there may be no performance feedback or delegation. The Managerial Leader at the skip level will often have to dip down to fill the missing work level, and this will be unsatisfactory to all parties. The work system will remain dysfunctional while this situation persists.

C may also represent the growth of an organisation into a new work level. The CEO leading the drive creates a vacuum behind her when stepping into the new, still emerging, and larger role. This missing work level is not filled by the executive team. The reason for this may be as a result of a number of design principles that were not considered or ignored. The outcome is that the new work level is not sustainable and the system collapses often with unfortunate results for stakeholders.

This is a common occurrence among Australian companies reaching out to play in work level VI and above. A recent example is The Insurance Australia Group (IAG), Australia's largest general insurer, which in the first decade of the 21st century, reached out under its dynamic CEO to embrace a new work level building and buying operations across multiple countries on different continents. The move was not sustained as the missing work level was not consolidated and the work system collapsed back on itself, with the CEO resigning.

Another example of C is an IT department which works on self-managed teams where work comes in, and the manager on the recommendation of his business analyst allocates works directly to developers, selecting who he thinks has the best skill set and leaves it up to that person to find a team and deliver the outcome. There is no context setting, integration, time and resource agreement, and erratic follow-up and monitoring. The developer is also not empowered with an authorised role relationship to form or lead a team and is reliant on good-will to accomplish their work. The IT department is seen as promising much, delivering little, inefficient, and failed to deliver time and time again. Its projects were continually late and over the budget. People avoided IT and workarounds sprung up.

D is an effective and well-designed reporting structure. Each role occupies one work level and reports to the role in the work level above. Each role has a quantitative and qualitatively different unique value adding focus with complimentary time spans of decision-making. There is no overlap or duplication, and each role has a clear set of authorities to match its accountabilities, regardless of whether it is vertical or a horizontal cross-functional role relationship (Principle 5).

This is natural hierarchy, not the rigid artificial disempowering power/control/prestige type of yesterday, but hierarchy around dealing with differing levels of work complexity.

So why is one role not reporting to another in the same work level necessary? If everyone reported to each other at the same level, who would

- set context and integrate the work and its tasks?
- prioritise work according to changing organisational needs?
- allocate resources and delegate? set authorities and accountabilities?
- monitor and review?
- conduct individual effectiveness review?
- have the authority to manage conflict?
- recognise and reward?
- be held accountable for expenditure of resources?
- provide coaching and recommend development?

In conclusion, a role occupies the level of work of the time span and UVA of its most complex task.

Principle 5: Empowering Role Relationships

To ensure effectiveness and performance, agree on authority levels for role relationships and ensure understanding to all stakeholders. This serves to link vertical and horizontal structure and work processes. It is the stage in the sequence where the Managerial Leader decides how to link and empower the work systems.

Authorised and communicated role relationships are the 'oil' for ensuring ongoing effective and healthy working relationships within these structures. Here the architect must, after considering and seeking all relevant input *decides how the roles are related . . .*

The *sequence of events* is as follows:

1. *Where are we going?* Decide where we are going, and what is our intent and our purpose for organising.
2. *How are we going to get there?* Determine what strategies are the most effective to accomplish the intent.
3. How will we organise ourselves? Decide the required functions, structures, and roles needed to deliver on the strategy.

4. *What work needs to be done?* Decide what actual work needs to be done.
5. *Decide how roles are related and what authority do they need to carry out their accountabilities?* It is important to ensure that authority match accountabilities. This determines how the system functions, and beware when restructuring or redesigning or adding in even one new role, it must always be done in context of how will it affect the flow of the work system.
6. *How do we recruit and deploy people effectively?* Deploy people who are inflow with the work challenges.
7. *How do we ensure effective leadership?* Ensure that Managerial Leadership competencies are taught for coherence and continuity.

What is Meant by Authority?

Authority is the power given to an individual by virtue of their role to expend resources, which may be financial, technical, and human to achieve an outcome.

What is Meant by Accountability?

Accountability is a situation where an individual can be called to account for his or her actions by another individual or body authorised to do so and to give recognition or censure to the individual for those actions. (Adapted from Jaques, 1996.)

What Is Meant by Responsibility?

This is often used in organisations but is difficult to define clearly and seems to cover both authority and accountability without being precise about what is explicit and what is implicit. We might define it as follows: *Responsibility is internal to one self, while a managerial leader holds his or her team accountable for effectiveness and performance.*

A Managerial Leader is accountable for deciding and setting clear authority in order to carry out accountabilities

- ***authorities***. This is dependent on the role type and the degree of authority required getting the job done. Managers rarely receive training in this important area and, as a result, can rise to senior levels without having a clear mental model on how to do it.
- ***accountabilities*** for what is required, in other words, what work is needed—the UVA and its KRAs.

There are *two basic role types* found in any organisational structure, and each of these has subsets with very specific authority levels.

The two basic roles are *line-management roles* and *specialist/ cross-functional roles*.

- There are a number of different line-management roles, each with its own authority levels.
- There are a number of different specialist roles, each with its own level of authority.
- A role can be a line manager as well as a specialist. They are not mutually exclusive.

All Managerial Leaders must be competent to

1. identify the role type they require to carry out the accountabilities.
2. set the authority level required to do so.
3. ensure *agreement between stakeholders* and *communicating this*, both horizontally and vertically to all involved.

Failure to do so means the following:

- The Managerial Leader cannot hold the incumbent accountable for personal effectiveness because he/she have not been given the clear authority to act.
- Across the value chain wasted resources, ineffective processes, delays and inefficiencies which result in poor customer service and increased costs manifested in damage to reputation, profit, image, and brand.
- Power politics and behaviours may emerge which undermine organisational values and result in unwanted and unwelcome outcomes.

- Growth of alternative work systems where achieving business outcomes has to be done through influencing and relying on goodwill. 'Workaround' are unauthorised systems that are needed to achieve business objectives because the work system is poorly designed and badly led, and people will go to great lengths to achieve objectives.

Consider a general manager (work level IV) trying to implement an innovative project supposedly approved at work level V and by the board but in which authority and accountabilities have not been agreed. The project is cross-functional and multinational in nature and works across an organisation of some 16,000 employees.

'I have found it really draining having to influence the need for a coordinated and aligned strategy across Australia and New Zealand. People say, 'yes, we need it', then go back into their silos and do what they want to do. There is no agreement at the top about this being needed and yet we are told to implement it.

'I have had a huge battle with one GM, and it became personal. He would not take my calls or respond to my emails. The short-term operational focus is frustrating, and there is no vision. There was such bad behaviour in the team. J, who runs a two-billion-dollar business, said he just does what Y tells him!

'I am also concerned because this project represents the only long-term project in the division as far as I am aware. It will change the way we go to market, and how we handle our reward and recognition. It will be a differentiating experience. It will provide one view, and it has not been done before. It has taken two years of influencing and $30 million in implementation costs. The company is so risk-averse that innovation is stifled. Silos and vested interests reign supreme'

'I am feeling so disheartened because it has been left up to me to influence my peers across the group, and if they say no or drag their heels, the project is stuck'

'Also, my team, on paper, is supposed to report to me, but I have no way of enforcing this, and their performance is still in the hands of their own

managers. They also cannot be held accountable for any outcomes as they have no authority and have to accomplish through favours, charisma, and cajoling. No one is accountable. Morale is low, and three people have resigned'

'My manager does her best, but she is not supported at the executive table. The CEO needs to take ownership of this or close it down, but he is never here. He is busy growing the company internationally and leaves it to the exec team to sort out details which they are not doing. It is now going to the project board for sign-off—twenty seven people have to sign off!'

'Then and only then, does it go to the main board to approve the next phase, which is eighteen months of development work'

What does accountability mean for effectiveness and performance?

First and foremost, it requires role clarity and authority to act effectively. It means 'earning one's keep', which means working at the level of effectiveness required of the role and the task.

It also means delivering on the tasks in a role for which the incumbent is held accountable. This is part of the equation for individual effectiveness. The rest of the equation is that the incumbent needs to have the appropriate knowledge, skills, experience and to be motivated by the work.

But it is more than that. 'Earning one's keep' means *making ambitious commitments and continually expanding them whenever possible and by striving to accurately support the overall team objective.*

What are the likely consequences for an employee who does 'earn his or her keep'?

- Personal gratification—'flow'
- Recognition and increased pay
- Developmental opportunities
- Enhanced promotability

Remember that the Managerial Leader's role is to ensure that the conditions are set for their team at the work level below to flourish and not to make it as difficult as possible to deliver on their KRAs as what happened in the case study.

Many Managerial Leaders do not know how to set these authorities, especially in large matrixes structures such as found in the financial services sector and in government agencies.

From an organisational perspective, accountability is the decision-making spine of an organisation and authority, the muscle. In Apple, that company so revered for innovation, secrecy, and delighting the customer, a 2011 Fortune article[34] reported that accountability is seen as a mindset that started with Jobs himself. 'At Apple, there is never any confusion who is responsible for what. Internal Applespeak even has a name for it, the 'DRI' or directly responsible (accountable) individual . . . any effective meeting at Apple will have an action list . . . next to each item will be the DRI.'

There are also few processes in the company, the article reported, but one of them is clarity of purpose of work emanating from a top-down command and control structure. In contrast to the belief that this works against flexibility and adaptability, Apple is nimble and creative. The main difference is that it focuses on a few things at a time. Jobs used to talk about the importance of picking the things you won't do. Key to this is that the article also stated that Jobs, when CEO, was not specifically involved in any one thing. This is an important point—while direction and priorities were set at the top, authority and accountability was given to those to get on with the work.

The two roles types are given below.

Line-management roles are vertical roles and are also known as *Task Assigning Role Relationships* (TARRS) which is most commonly the manager with a team of direct reports who has the authority to assign tasks directly or delegate them. There are five different line-management roles that have been identified and researched.

Cross-functional and specialist roles are those roles which do not have leadership requirements. Seven different *Task Initiating Role Relationships* (TIRRS) have been identified. At the one end of the continuum, the authority level is low. A can go to B for advice but does not need to heed it. At the other end of the continuum, authority can be the same as a line manager. In such a case, A can tell B to stop, and B must stop.

The difference lies in the level of authority a role requires to carry out its accountabilities.

Minimum Managerial Authorities

Line-management roles must have certain Minimum Managerial Authorities and here's why . . .

If A is going to hold B accountable for the output of C, then B must have a minimum set of authority to manage C without interference from A.

This is referred to as Managerial Authority, and the reason for this is, you cannot hold B accountable for the performance of C as they do have the authority to take certain actions.

Jaques referred to this Minimum Managerial Authority as *VARI* and that means

- *The right to veto an appointment (V)*
  (The manager cannot be held accountable for the performance of someone who is appointed to his or her team without their agreement. The reason for this is that the new team member may not have the right background or the technical knowledge, skills, or experience to do the work.)

- *Decide what tasks to assign (A)*
  This is the right to assign tasks, to add or lessen task load, to prioritise, and to delegate tasks.

- *The right to reward, recognise, review, or recommend (R)*

The manager has the authority to reward team members which may be written, on the spot, verbal, merit, and increase with agreed limits (it undermines managerial authority to leave this up to committees), recommend internal or external training or development and assignment to new special projects within the manager's work system.

However issues like promotion, changes to pay grades, or pay bands cannot be decided and must be 'recommended' to the level above manager who has that type of authority. This is the team member's MoR, and the MoR has VARI of a different nature.

- *Initiate transfer from a role (I)*
  Like with pay and promotion, the manager does not have the right to 'decide' to move someone from his or team, they have to 'recommend'. The right to decide these matters (dismissal, appeal, assess career potential etc.) lies with their manager at the next level, the MoR. Removal from the role may mean transfer to a different role, to a project or exiting due to repeated poor performance.

Line-Management Roles.

There are five subsets in line-management roles, each with different authorities and accountabilities.

Table 3 lays out the five role types, which are indicated across the top, running horizontally left to right. VARI is indicated vertically and each role type is shown with the authority to decide (D) or to recommend only (R). It is worth pointing out how the MoR and manager have a complimentary set of authorities and accountabilities and that the MoR has no authority in the day-to-day management of direct reports. On the far left, the role of supervisor is shown with mostly recommend authority.

Table 3: **Line-management role authorities**

D=Decide R=Recommend

Accountabilities & Authorities	MoR	Mgr	PM	PL	Supervisor
Veto appointment	D	D	D	D	R
Induct & set context	-	D	D	-	R
Set type of tasks	-	D	D	-	R
Assign tasks	-	D	D	D	D
Coach & train	-	D	D	-	R
+/- tasks	-	D	D	-	D
Verbal recognition	-	D	D	-	D
Recorded recognition	-	D	R	-	R
Expand/reduce task type	-	D	R	-	R
positive or negative pay change	-	D	R	-	R
Initiate transfer from role	-	D	D	D	R
Assess career potential/mentor	D	R	-	-	R
Adjust pay band	D	R	-	-	R
+ve or -ve transfers	D	R	-	-	R
Promote/demote	D	R	-	-	R
Dismiss	D	R	-	-	R
Appeal	D	-	-	-	-

With Acknowledgement. Requisite Organisation.1987,1996. PeopleFit Australasia 2006.

1. *The Manager:* Managerial Leadership roles have full VARI, and these role types are found from work level II to VII. At work level II, we find the first full Managerial Leaders with VARI authority. They are known as Front-Line Managers (FLM).

The manager has to plan how to get their work done, and this cannot be delegated. This is their UVA, and while they may obtain advice and input from various parties, it is their accountability. They can delegate work only when they have worked out what must be done by whom and when. Then work can be delegated and tasks assigned. This is the key part of the authority of the role—*assigning work and/or authorising work.*

The manager needs to review regularly and monitor performance and reward or take corrective action as appropriate.

2. *The Supervisor:* This is the Front-Line Manager's (FLM) assistant, and they do not have full VARI. It is a support role with limited authority and accountability for daily supervision. The supervisor may also provide verbal recognition and on-the-job coaching. The supervisor role is a high level I role and is accountable for managing self and a team on a daily basis. This level of work often abounds with multiple titles—team leaders, supervisors, assistant team leaders, and service managers. This is a common role where a FLM manages large groups such as in a call centre.
3. *The Project Manager (PM):* The project manager has almost the same level of authority as the manager with regard to those assigned to the project team, except that he or she cannot deal with performance issues where the team is of less than six months duration. This is why the set-up of appropriate project boards or steering committees who have authority to assign their people to the project is critical for shorter duration projects.

If the project runs for more than six months, the project team member should be transferred to become a direct report. This is because the regular manager cannot have view of the individual's performance over such a period of time and therefore cannot be held accountable, which means that they cannot make comments on the incumbents' individual effectiveness. In companies where project work plays a major part, the authority of project managers needs to be carefully considered in terms of training them in an effective team management process, and project managers are appointed with the capability to handle the level of work of the project.

4. *The Project Leader (champion):* This is peer-to-peer management, such as a group of senior managers or general managers who have to work together and where one has been appointed by the CEO as project leader.
5. *The Manager Once Removed MoR:* As mentioned above, this is an important role with a different set of complimentary authorities and accountabilities to a manager. While many organisations

realise the importance of this role, few have actively given it the appropriate accountabilities or authority it requires.

Figure 12 illustrates the broad areas of authority and accountability. The MoR is accountable and has the authority to ensure quality of leadership through fairness of processes, such as hearing appeals, promotion or dismissal and deciding the career for his or her skip level reports (Reports Once Removed—RoR).

The MoR has a strong interest in developing the talent pool and in succession planning. He or she has the right to veto an appointment of RoRs, and this is a shared authority with his direct report (see Table 3. They both have veto rights). The reason for this is that he or she will choose successors from that talent pool and in time become their direct reports. Thus they have responsibility for ensuring a rich talent pool. The MoR plays an important part in the performance review cycle, ensuring that the manager's treatment of his or her direct report is even-handed and is fair and consistent with values.

The MoR is also vitally interested in developing a successor for his or direct reports, and in the performance review, where he or she signs off on their managers assessment, the opportunity should be presented to discuss future career prospects as the MoR has a wider view of the organisation, the function, and its current and future needs.

The MoR also decides on structure at the RoR level, specifically how many subordinate roles there will be, their unique value add (UVA), and if it is high, mid, or low with the level (time-span dependent). There are major resourcing implications for this type of decision. The MoR has no part in daily managerial activities of the RoR; for example, it is the manager's role to decide what tasks they assign to their reports.

Figure 12: **The MoR accountabilities**

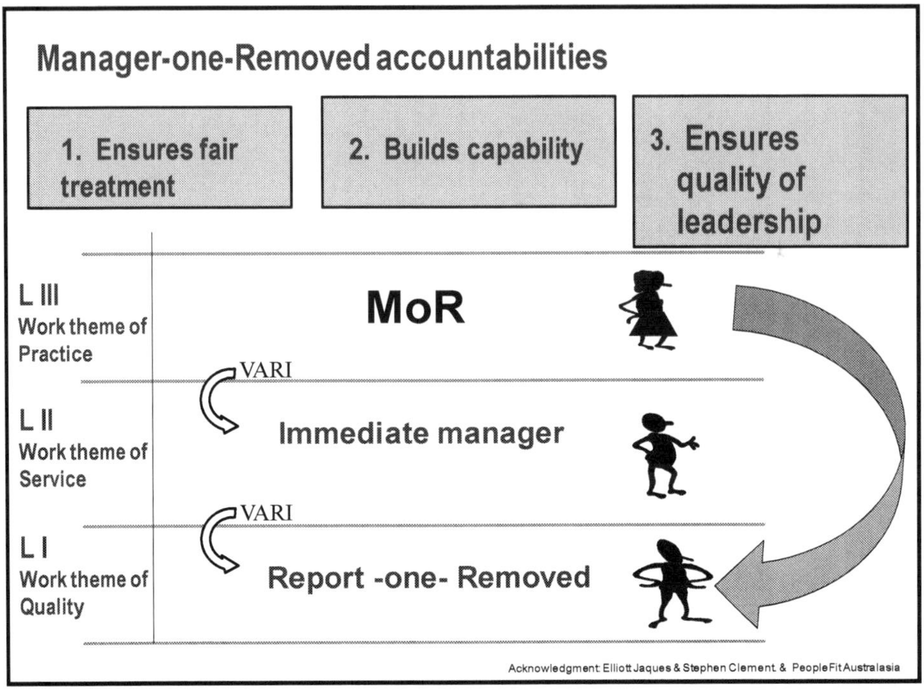

The MoR also has the authority to sign off on cross-functional role authority in order to ensure that the work flow is integrated across functions. It is the MoR who is accountable to ensure that these authorities and accountabilities are communicated to all relevant parties.

In summary, the MoR must create the conditions for the levels below to flourish, in order to add their unique value, and to ensure consistent standards in leadership, decision-making authority, and operational effectiveness.

- Build the talent pool and ensure that succession planning is in place. (Answering the question, what is my future for RoRs?) Remember the veto authority for promotions is shared with the manager.
- Ensure fair treatment and review of decision where appropriate.
- Ensure consistency of leadership and its quality at the level below his or her direct reports.
- Setting structure and role alignment.

Figure 13 below indicates the passage of leadership through each work level and by domain. *Excellence* is the leadership mantra of the value added domain. Since it can be measured, it is often tangible and has a clear outcome. In the Innovative Domain, it is less tangible, and the outcome is less certain, but it is about creating *anticipation* for the promises of the desired future. It is pragmatic, yet inspirational and striving.

While for the Values Domain, the theme of leadership is *tolerance* for diversity, the unknown, the fact is there is often little we can do to define the desired outcomes or the attitude of different players. It is about keeping doors open and dialogue flowing.

Figure 13: **Passage of leadership**

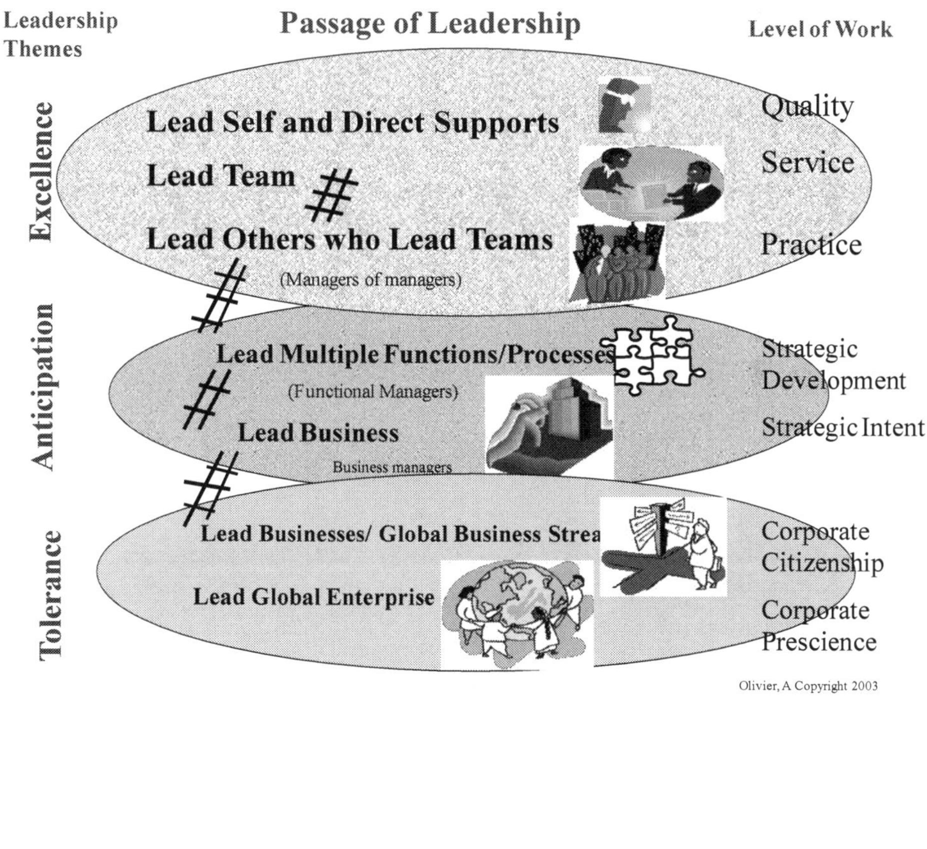

Specialist and Cross-Functional Support Roles

What do we need to be clear about?

The most common manager-employee relationship is that of a line manager role or Task Assigning Role Relationship (TARR) in which the Managerial Leaders have the authority to assign work to their direct report.

However, there are many functions across the organisation that require people and teams to work together, usually beginning with one party requesting an action from another party. They are in such a case, *initiating a task for someone who does not directly report to them.*

If a role is authorised to do this, then it is cross-functional role or a *Task Initiating Role Relationship* (TIRR). The key question is—how to authorise a role to initiate tasks from others.

Cross-functional and specialist roles relationships do not have leadership authority or accountability. They work across roles and may work across departmental/functional boundaries within a work system or across multiple work systems. They usually provide expertise or specialist services. Common examples are HR, risk management, internal audit, IT, public affairs, project office, finance, and facilities.

This is often an area of frustration in many organisations, and it is, therefore, a key part of creating competitive advantage if done well.

These roles have the authority to initiate tasks or provide services on request but cannot directly assign work to others through a direct reporting relationship. In some cases, they may also be line managers in their right or sole contributors. An HR Manager may provide an advisory role to many in the organisation, but they are line mangers to their own direct reports, with leadership accountability.

However, it is these cross functional roles that are often the most problematic and stressful. Line managers who have such roles reporting to them must ensure clear authority and accountability is not only set but *communicated, understood, and agreed* by all relevant parties.

There are seven task initiating roles types, ranged along a continuum from little authority to maximum authority (on par with a line manager).

See Table 4.

In today's increasingly complex and integrated world, organisations need effective cross-functional integration. Seamless integration is required, and as such we have seen the evolution of matrix structures as an attempt to manage this need. All sorts of topsy have risen in the search for more organic 'networked' structures.

By clearly defining cross-functional/specialist role relationships and communicating them regularly, an organisation can reduce employee frustration, improve productivity, and create an effective workplace, real or virtual, across functional areas and geographical distance.

Obligations of Service Providing Functions

A service-providing function such as IT, finance, and HR will often receive work via the business initiating a task with them; effectively, the business has 'Service-Getting' authority over these areas.

It is the obligation of these areas to be able to respond to the business in a timely manner as to *when and at what cost* they would be able to complete the requested task. Without this, the business is not able to make decisions on how they will spend their resources. There will naturally be times when the business will require the work to be completed in a shorter timeframe or in a different way to how it was advised, and flexibility from the service-proving area might not be possible.

In these situations, it is critical that the issue be raised between the MoRs as a scheduling issue, *not as a performance issue*. It is not a criticism, and if there are perceived issues with performance, this should be handled in a different forum. If the MoRs can't agree, this suggests that clarity is required in terms of business priorities, and a discussion should occur at a higher level until this is clear.

Table 4: **Specialist/non-managerial role authorities**

A=Initiator B=Responder

Increasing Authority Levels ←

Accountabilities & Authorities / Role Types	Prescribe (not common)	Audit	Coordinate	Monitor	Service getting (Most Common Type)	Collateral	Advisory
A can instruct B to do something	✓	–	–	–	✓	–	–
A can instruct B to stop & B stops	✓	✓	–	–	–	–	–
A can instruct B to delay & B delays	✓	✓	✓	✓	–	–	–
A and B disagree . A decides	✓	✓	–	–	–	–	–
A can be informed about B's work	✓	✓	✓	✓	–	✓	–
A can have access to persuade B	✓	✓	✓	✓	–	✓	–
A can have access to explain to B	✓	✓	✓	✓	–	✓	✓
A can call coordinative meetings with Bs	–	–	✓	–	–	–	–
A can report higher about B	✓	✓	✓	✓	✓	–	–
If A and B disagree, they do what their immediate manager would want	–	–	✓	–	✓	✓	–

With Acknowledgements. Requisite Organisation. 1987,1996 & PeopleFit Australasia 2006.

A good follow-up resource on role types is in *The Practice of Managerial Leadership* by Nancy R. Lee who describes these roles in detail.[35] The book is available at Amazon.com.

Practical Advice:
Setting Up Cross-Functional Roles Across the Organisation

Sales, product manufacturing, transactions, and many other processes flow across business units, linking geographical locations, and this involve a range of different roles, sometimes at different work levels. Employees may be involved in one part of a business process that impacts a number of different functions and have authorised role relationships with other roles in those other functions who do not report to them.

Specialists and service roles may work within a function or provide services to multiple clients across the organisation. These non-managerial roles also require authorised role relationships in their interactions with others to respond to or initiate work.

This is a real stumbling point in many organisations, and when poorly done or 'left up to them to sort it out', it results in situations that lead to situations such as

- 'I don't know who is accountable. They have both made requests and then tell me different things.'
- 'This place works too much in silos.'
- 'That area has the same role as my area.'
- 'I can't get any response from that area, so I can't do my job.'
- 'I have no authority to get any action, and you can see what is wrong.'
- 'They are too busy all the time.'
- 'I feel that should be addressed, but I am ignored.'
- 'It is left up to me to get results through influencing.'
- 'There is no planning, no coordination.'
- 'They don't share information, and I don't know what is going on.'

Examples

Case Study 1

Let us return to that large, cross-functional and multinational project described by the frustrated general manager (p. 60). Here are comments from other employees involved in that project who were in cross-functional roles.

My success is dependent on others, and what is important to me is not important to them. The KPIs are not aligned, and they have a huge impact on whether I achieve my objectives. Only way I can make progress is to influence and go and see them and learning different ways to achieve outcomes. I have no authority, and they don't have to do or even help with our key issues.

In the structure, there is also lack of role clarity—we do our best, and everyone has an opinion on how to run it. They should rather focus on getting the strategy right and then have accountability clearly set out for delivery.

And another employee involved with the same project said, *'We have stakeholder briefs, and there is not time to discuss changes. They just happen, and it is a continual period of change over long period of time with insufficient engagement, and problems get compounded. Its rush, rush, rush, but nothing gets signed off, and no progress is made or at least so it seems to me . . . There is little to prove progress, and it's such a pity. This is a really revolutionary idea and would add huge value to our offerings nationwide and be a real benefit to customers.'*

In the above example, there should have been clear authority and accountability given to the project manager as per Table 4, and this communicated to all the executive level members and stakeholders. She should have had a permanent team assigned to her with their authority and accountability made clear, and this communicated to the organisation. TIRR roles should have been negotiated, agreed, and communicated. The project eventually folded, wasting tens of millions of dollars with many victims and few beneficiaries.[36]

Case Study 2

A risk manager (B) is held accountable by her manager (A) for ensuring risk is managed appropriately throughout the organisation. In order for B to be effective, she has to have the appropriate level of authority agreed upon by A with his peers and then communicated to the organisation and recorded in the PD and in other relevant governance documentation.

The role type for this specialist role is one that doesn't just require other managers and their staff to respond to B. It may also require them to change their work and processes if required to achieve appropriate management of risk.

In other words, *B needs the authority to be able to initiate work from people who do not report to them*. To do this, A needs to set up a Task Initiating Role Relationship and discuss this with his group of peers. They can then accept A's requirement for an *Audit role authority,* and it is added into the PD. A's boss, as MoR, is accountable for setting structure at B's level, so they will need to get her approval for the arrangements or resolve any issues that may arise.

Let us look at the Risk Manager (B) now. B is also a manager in her own right and has a team of five direct reports (Cs), some of whom have reports (D). She is thus both a line manager (TARR) to Cs and MoR to D. In addition to this, she also acts a specialist working across the organisation with an 'Audit' level of authority (see Figure 14 for details of that authority).

Figure 14: **Case study 2—a matrix of working relationships**

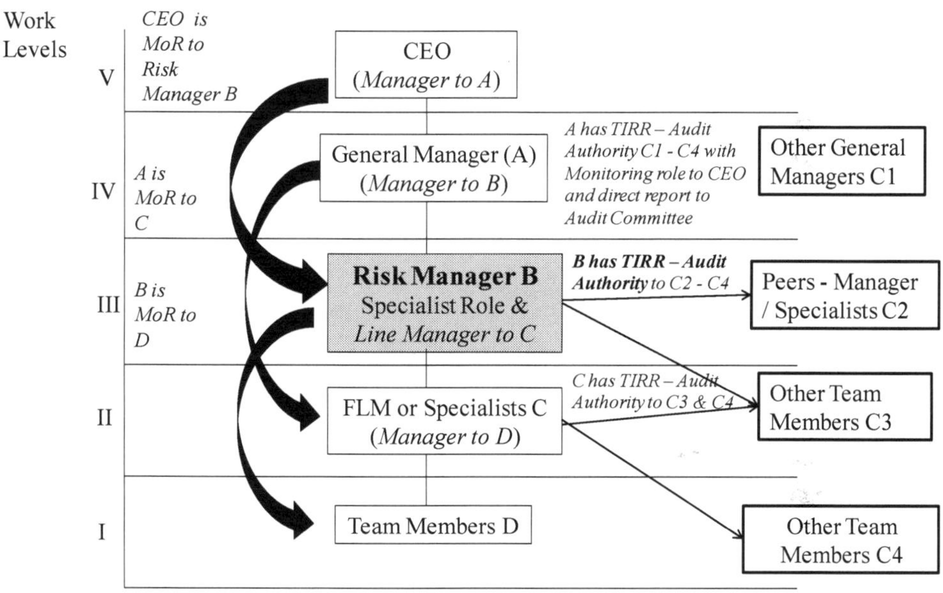

Roles Types, Reporting Distance and Authority Levels

A Suggested Process for Establishing TIRR Role Authorities

A and his peers, let us call them the general managers at work level IV, came to agreement on the purpose of their teams and that covered the accountability of their team managers. They discussed each role and came to an agreement on the TIRR authorities required in order to allow each manager to achieve what they will be accountable for. This is then included into the PD of each person and to their team members as required and briefed as appropriate.

Tools

- Sheet—'Non-managerial role authorities (TIRRs)' (see Table 4 above)
- Business plan of each area
- PDs

How It's Done

1. The general managers (including A) involved get together to discuss the purpose of the teams that are involved and the subsequent accountability of the manager of each team of which B is one.

   This is an important process and must be completed so that there is agreement and understanding. All Managerial Leaders in work level III *and above* need to be competent in setting *structure* and *alignment* to business purpose. This is a core competency of business leadership and reserved for work level III and above.

   In contrast, *all* Managerial Leaders need to understand the different role types and how to allocate authority and accountability. Not many institutions teach this as core competencies, and as a result, managers need to learn by trial and experience. No wonder this is such a problematic area!

   Question: Why is work level III the starting point of accountability for setting structure and work alignment?

   Answer: Because this is the first level where the MoR role is found, and one of its core accountabilities is approving structure and roles and authority levels.

2. Each GM clearly defines on paper what their manager is accountable for, then asks that manager what authority they would require,

with regard to other areas, in order to get other achieve this. This is done by going through the TIRR Sheet (see section below).

3. The GMs involved get together again to discuss and agree the proposed types of TIRR authority, using examples to explain how it would work. Disagreement must be considered in the light of each team's overall purpose, and if agreement can't be reached, it needs to be referred up to the chief executive.

   If the GMs cannot agree on issues such as the purpose, authority, and accountability of a team, it must be referred up to the chief executive officer to be resolved.

   Question: Why the CEO?

   Answer: She is the MoR to B (see Figure 14).

   Managers may be part of this discussion if appropriate, but these discussions are often very sensitive. It may be better for the GMs to agree before discussing with their reports.

4. Once TIRR authorities are agreed, these are included in each manager's PD. This process is then repeated as required down through the work levels.

Using the TIRR sheet

The level of authority is at the highest on the left side of the sheet (Prescribe), decreasing as the columns go to the right. (Refer Table 4.)

- It is generally advisable to agree on the minimal authority required for initiating tasks in others; for example, if Coordinate authority is sufficient, there is no need to argue for Audit authority.
- Working through requires constant referring back to what the person asking for the authority is held accountable for.
- If disagreement can't be resolved, it is critical that these be referred up and not decided on a personality basis.

- End result is 'Boss, for me to do what you're holding me accountable for doing, I'm going to need (TIRR Authority type) authority regarding (department/role).'

Across the Organisation

TIRR roles are cross functional Levels of work, and line-management roles address vertical structure. Cross-functional roles address horizontal structure and process flows, cutting across departments and line-management-reporting structures.

Understanding the flow of process is important in aligning TIRR roles. For example, in a large Conference and Event Centre, there is a process that runs across all the functional areas of operation. The HR team with the director of the centre charted the flow of work.

Vertically, it is a three-tier department reporting into a general manager at work level IV. The department employs 385 people, fractionally more than the optimal size but that is due to demand, which sees many casuals employed as waitrons.

There are three separate sections reporting to the director, namely a Convention and Events Sales Manager (who gets the business), a Convention and Events Manager (who organises the event in liaison with the client and suppliers), and a Convention Operations Manager (who does the actual event).

Each of these managers are line managers in their own right with direct reports, but some of their direct reports have to work with colleagues in the other departments to make the event happen and delight the client.

Work is sought by the Business Development Manager. Hosting a convention is agreed upon with a new client. The event details are recorded and passed on to an Event Manager who coordinates the requirements with the client and suppliers and internal functions. The deal is closed, and she passes the event requirements to the Operations department, who keeps the Event Manager informed. Eventually, the convention goes off as agreed. After the event is closed off by accounts, the Events Manager is required to follow-up with the client as to their satisfaction. Each of these cross-functionally related roles require their own authority requirements to deliver on their accountabilities.

An analysis of the value chain cross-functionally in Figure 15 showed that the level III functional managers were not involved in cross-functional process flow and only operated in their silos to ensure their part of the value chain was carried out effectively. This absence of work level III 'cost control', 'system efficacy', quality, and service management meant that business opportunities had been lost. The gap between what was promised and what was delivered was not always ideal, and there was no link back to business development. Also, the Operations department was not always fully in the loop on the status of events.

Importantly, the system was not effective and employee frustration was high as the authority levels and cross-functional role types had not been agreed between the level III managers and the GM and communicated across the work system.

Figure 15: **Process flow across convention and events centre**

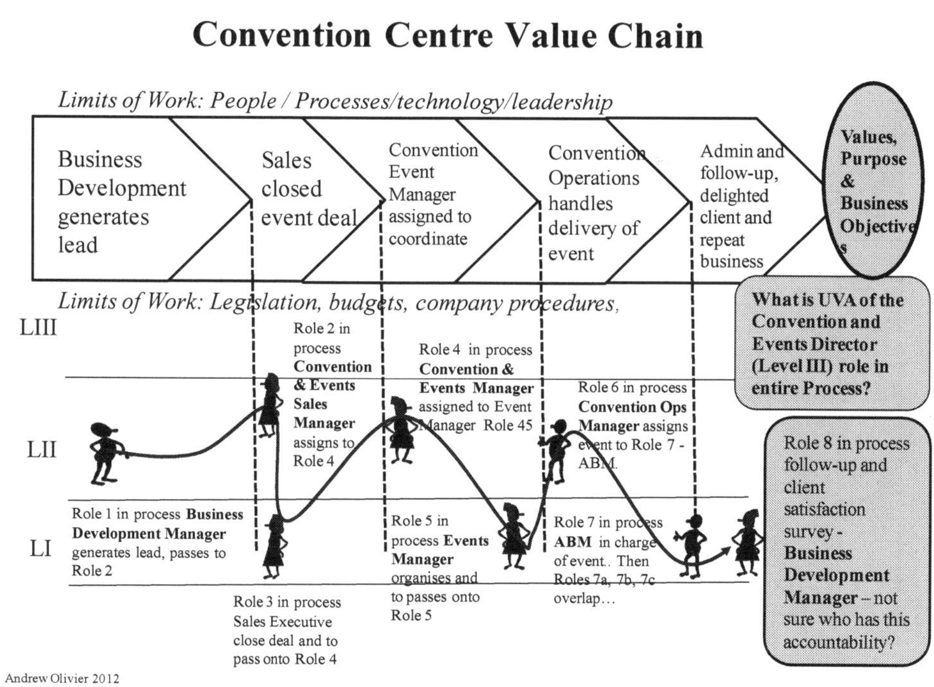

Principle 6: Matching Individual Capability to Role Complexity

An individual appointed into a role must have the current actual capability *at that given point in time* to carry out the level of work complexity required.

The provision of career paths is not part of the principles of design.

Principle 6 is generic such that it applies to all roles at all work levels, but for senior management, this is essential not only for effective healthy work structures but for the successful delivery of workable strategies as well.

The more complex the role (e.g. group CEOs, CEOs, MDs, GMs, vice-presidents, and senior managers), the greater the risk to delivery and to profitability, image, and reputation if the appointed individual operates at too low or too high a level.

Current Actual Capability (CAC) refers *to the level of work where a person can be effectively deployed and where he or she can actually operate successfully.*

A general principle *is people grow or shrink their roles and tasks to the current level of work in which they are most comfortable and in which they feel 'in flow'.*

Current Actual Capability—is a function of a number of interrelated factors.

The *Cognitive Power* (CP) of the individual is the foundation of the individual's current level of work ability and a guide to their future potential levels of work. CP is defined *as the potential strength of cognitive processes in a person and is therefore the maximum level of task complexity that someone can handle at any give point in his or her development.*

CP, in essence, refers to an individual's cognitive ability to assimilate data and information and to exercise sound judgment in the face of ambiguity and uncertainty. Research shows that this unfolds at different but predictable rates with maturity and varies from person to person. The exercise of judgment becomes more and more important when the facts and figures stop short of obvious solutions, and the increase in variables make decision-making increasingly difficult.

Research by Jaques and others have shown there are a number of growth modes that govern human capability, and it is possible to accurately match an individual's cognitive capability with a work level and *predict* when he or she may move to the next work level, thus allowing effective talent management.

Cognitive capability and how it influences the growth of an organisation is illustrated in Section II with the case studies of Virgin, Grameen Bank, Facebook, and Executive Outcomes.

Information on CP may be derived from different methods some of which are listed here:

- Capability interviews (externally delivered appreciation/ assessments—such as the Complexity Navigation Process(CIP), Career Path Appreciation, Modified Career Path Appreciation, the Initial Recruitment Interview Schedule (IRIS), the Working Journey Interview, or any form of predictive potential assessment derived from this model)
- The judgment of the direct manager and that of MoR as to their current performance and their potential to perform at high-level roles. This assessment should be substantiated by individual effectiveness/performance reports, stretch assignments, acting roles at the next work level, and reviews.
- Through a deliberate, calibrated process such as Rapid Talent Pool Evaluation.[37]

Knowing an individual's CP is essential for effective and healthy work systems. However, it is *one* of a number of other factors, and while it cannot be learnt or obtained, it does not on its own allow for effective deployment. The following factors also have to be considered.

The second key factor required is having the *knowledge, skills, and experience* (K/S/E) to be effective in that role in that work level. This can be obtained from records, tests, qualifications, and work history. This, in contrast to CP, can be learned, obtained, or developed. K/S/E needs continual updating and diversity.

The third factor is whether the person *values* (V) the work; whether it is work that engenders a commitment to the work, be it a passion, necessity or interest. Information on this can be obtained from opinions and interviews and testimonials.

The fourth factor is having the *wisdom* (Wi, also known as EQ) to handle relationships and work so that the accumulation of experience is additive and allows for the growth of positive relationships even when situations are not optimal. This can be obtained from opinions and interviews such as 180 or 360 evaluations.

The last factor is that personality, referred to as *temperament* (T), is *not* an issue in a well-led structure. Personalities get out of control when a work system is not well led and requisitely constructed; e.g. there are too many managerial or supervisory levels. T in a requisite leadership structure is not an issue unless there are psychological problems with the individual. T is governed by requisite structure (correct levels, clearly defined accountabilities and authorities). This can be obtained from opinions and interviews. Far too much effort is focused in on identifying and pandering to T when the core competencies of Managerial Leadership are ignored. T is an issue only when there are other more deep-rooted factors at play.

Thus having the *Current Actual Capability* (CAC) to be effective in a role may be summarised as a function of having the *Cognitive Power* (CP) required for the level of work complexity plus having the appropriate *knowledge, skills, and experience (K/S/E)* needed in the role plus *valuing* the work (V) plus having the *wisdom (W)* to deal with complex relationships.

However, it is not always necessary or possible that a candidate will have the K/S/E for the role but having the CP is a requisite requirement. Knowledge, skills, and experience can be learned on the job or through development interventions; CP cannot.

By deploying people whose current actual capability is aligned with the level-of-work complexity required for their role, one is setting up the core requirements of a healthy work system.

Principle 7: Ensuring Leadership Coherence

Ensure Managerial Leadership **Competence**: Create coherence through competence by ensuring that all Managerial Leaders operate using these principles and those that make up the approach of effective leadership called RO.

Getting work levels aligned to strategy, UVAs, and time spans will not mean much if it remains a theory. Everyday practices needs to ensure work is taking place at the right level for driving outcomes.

To hold the work-systems integrity, one must ensure that the Managerial Leadership cadre understands these seven principles and are able to apply them effortlessly. This can only be done through a coherent leadership development programme.

The seven principles are part of an integral approach for effective managerial leadership for growing successful ventures and effective leadership of organisations of all sizes. This means effective managerial leadership competence is required in all roles where a manager is held accountable for their own outputs (their own UVA particular to their level), outputs of their team, and in building and leading that team to achieve agreed business outcomes.

All senior managers from level III upwards need to know how to do the following:

- Set a strategy to achieve a business outcome—remembering Principle 1 which states that the business purpose will set the required level of work complexity. The executive needs to know how many work levels are required, and this is ascertained by the understanding the most complex task in the strategy. They also need to understand the sequence of events to follow in designing structure.

- Build scale using the team (MKU) and three-tier structure (MRU) as the fundamental building blocks.
- Write and maintain effective PDs which describe multiple roles where appropriate and are accurate descriptions of the work process with each PD having a UVA and identified time span. PDs are a system of work that documents the process of work flow and authorises role relationships.
- Ensure the right reporting distance between roles at different work levels so that there is clear authority for empowerment.
- Work cooperatively in ensuring the alignment of processes and systems and projects so that role relationships are authorised and communicated. This means roles vertically and horizontally are linked and empowered by the appropriate authority needed to carry out given accountabilities in order to get the job done, and *that this is communicated.* Failure to do this effectively is tantamount to setting up the team to fail, blow out budgets and timelines.
- Build in the practices of the MoR function. It has specific role authorities which are unique to the role and ensures coherence of structure and roles, quality of leadership, and the building talent pool robustness.
- Carry out the MoR role. The MoR is the exemplar of organisational values. The MoR ensures fairness of appeals and decisions which are escalated. Review should be built into performance appraisals to ensure this, and it is only the MoR who can provide insight on their longer term prospects of his RoR within the company.

In addition to these key and basic effective managerial skills, ***all*** Managerial Leaders from work level II to work level VII must be competent at the following:

- Building and leading a team so that all are competent, capable, and committed to move in the direction set. Managers need a team-work process in which team leaders lead, and they need to understand Principle 3.
- Setting context for work and integration of tasks for their team so that work is prioritised and resources allocated in the shifting milieu of work.

- Carry out Principle 5 by cascading authority in a planned and logical manner. In other words, being able to set authorities and accountabilities for their team and to ensure that all newcomers understand their role and its authority and accountability.
- Effective tasking is a skill and is not something all managers are inherently good at doing. They can be trained in this, and by understanding how to effectively task, *they allocate work at the right work level and in line with the team members' capability.* There are a number of requirements that need to be fulfilled in drafting up an effective task. Key amongst that is complying with Principle 6—of matching individual capability to role complexity and that the task's complexity is fully understood (Principle 3).
- Communication, conflict management and resolution, and understanding themselves and their team.

These competencies are critical to building trust and building an organisation geared to perform. (For more information on Principle 7, refer to Services offered in support of this book)

Summary

The seven principles for designing organisational structure are given below.

Principle 1: Business Intent and Required Complexity

How many work levels are needed to deliver the organisation's purpose? There are a maximum of seven levels of work, and each deals with an increase in work complexity and offers a unique value add. This dimension is essential for vertical structural design and appears as a global design requirement in all natural hierarchies.

Principle 2: Optimal Size

There is a design blueprint for all functions that starts with the team and which has a scalable three-tier structure. There is an optimal company size based on the very human characteristic of knowing 'faces' and 'names', and it is scalable.

Principle 3: Making Decisions equals Work

Decide what work needs to be done to achieve the strategic intent/work purpose. Analyse the tasks to understand the work level. The 'level' can be measured by its time span of decision-making—the maximum time it takes to complete the most complex task. Thus the number of levels required is determined by the most complex task.

Principle 4: Reporting Distance

One role must not report to another in the same level of work to avoid duplications and overlaps. Requisite distance empowers structures and allows authorised role relationships to work effectively. Utilise financial and human capital effectively.

Principle 5: Empowering Role Relationships

Agree on authority levels of role relationships and ensure understanding. Understanding role types and their authority is important as it empowers structure and processes horizontally. This is both horizontal and vertical design dimensions. There is a sequence of events in assigning authority and role relationships.

Principle 6: Matching Individual Capability to Role Complexity

Appoint people to the role who can handle the level of work complexity. An individual appointed into a role must have the current actual capability at that given point in time to carry out the level of work complexity required.

Principle 7: Ensuring Leadership Coherence

Everyday practices needs to ensure that work is taking place at the right level for driving outcomes. Ensure coherence through competence to apply these principles, using a common language of understanding and common practices of Managerial Leadership.

SECTION II

The Seven Levels of Work Complexity

A Closer Examination of the Vertical Dimension With Illustrative Stories

An Overview of the Work Domains[38]

Figure 16: **Domains and levels of work**

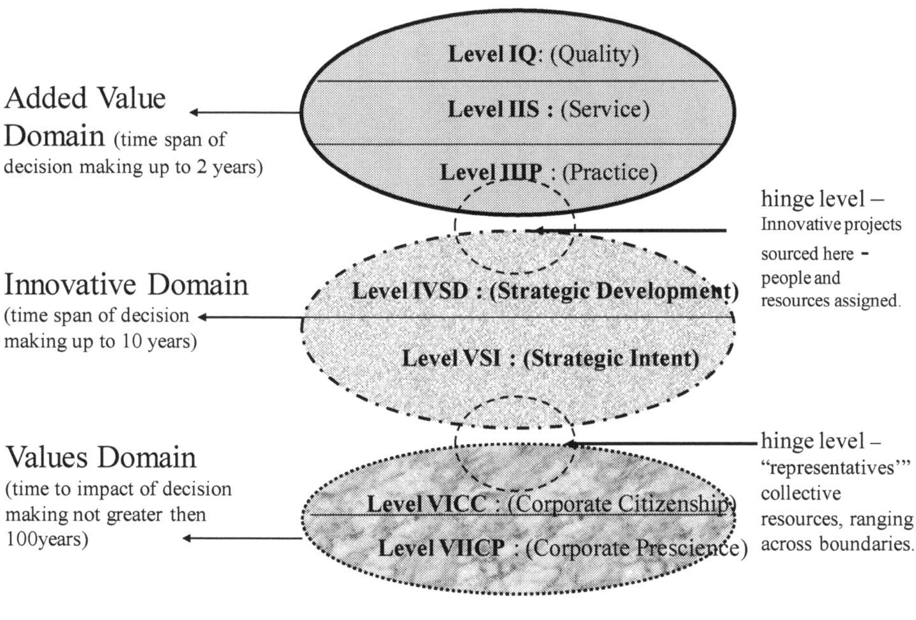

Acknowledgments ; Jaques, Stamp and Hoebeke. Adapted from the Working Journey©, Andrew Olivier 2012.

The Added Value Domain

These first three levels are about operational work.

This domain and its three levels of endeavour are largely concerned with operational work and the delivery of services, manufacturing of goods, and extraction of resources. Work here is about 'the how' and doing work in the most cost-effective and efficient manner.

This domain is about 'doing'. This is where operational efficiency, productivity, and industry expertise are critical. It is the primary locus of activity for goal-directed human endeavours, and the leadership theme is *excellence*.

The work is about serving a known client base with known products and services. It is concerned with asking whether the systems, processes, and procedures are still doing what they should be doing and whether there is a possibility of doing them more effectively.

In these first three levels of contribution, we find all sorts of endeavours, ranging from the corner café to mining operations, supermarkets, call centres, retail outlets, fast food chains, construction, service centres for insurance, banking operations, hubs for transport, and military units—all tasked with producing or making calls on given and known targets or objectives, using known methods, procedures, and systems.

It is important to note that this work domain starts establishing contacts with other work systems internally and externally from work level II. This may be through professional associations. At work level III, this is in the form of benchmarks, searching for world's best practices, following, and maybe emulating what competitors are doing and where we can be better and offer new services around known products to the known client base at the same or better cost.

Essentially, work in this domain is about transforming a relatively standard or given set of requirements of existing customers into outputs, whereby value is added for the shareholders and employees but not necessarily for all stakeholders.

Uncertainty and ambiguity need to be driven out of the system so that the system operates as faultlessly as possible; although creativity is always required at all work levels.

Leadership is about striving for continual improvement and for excellence in all areas. The levels in this domain are not responsible for committing resources or making decisions about introducing new products and services. Part of their work through approaches such as CRM and data mining is to understand the known client base and product range and to test out potential interest to assist positioning in the market. Very often, suggestions for improvement, new ideas, and new products originate from this domain and its vibrant interactions.

The Added Value Domain overlaps with the Innovative Domain at the top end of work level III which is focused on implementing or testing out new new systems and products which may impact the future.

The Innovative Domain

This domain and its two work levels are commonly referred to as executive work and form the top end of the individual company or that of a large organisational divisional structure. It may represent a discrete work entity or a major division of a corporate group. This could include national or multinational units and may represent a product stream or a full standalone company. Here, the magnificence of the whole game in which one is contextualised becomes apparent.

The two levels (IV and V) are to do with shaping the organisation's future and guiding it as a unified whole; as such they represent a different type of work to the Added Value Domain both quantitatively and qualitatively. They are about discovering and creating innovations and renewals for the future through consciously creating the future. It is a proactive domain, and leadership is future focussed but with a tight focus on the success of current operations in the first three work levels.

Substantial resources may be committed to new and existing endeavours. Poor judgement can be significantly costly as the vulnerabilities may be great. This domain is subject to powerful forces from a rapidly changing external environment. The forces that buffet this domain have intensified as a result of 'wide time', globalism, consumerism, and its empowering and all-pervasive technologies.

Global competitiveness, changed regulatory environments, environmental degradation, and increased social responsibility are making this work domain a more contentious place. Some argue that the impacts of the last century are only just beginning to make their presence felt.

A primary part of this role is to offer shelter to the domain below and to create the conditions for it to grow with purpose and enthusiasm. The outward-facing, public component of work in this domain continues to increase in importance.

Here uncertainty and ambiguity represent key resources both as vulnerability and as opportunity. It is the only resource, which, if used and understood, represents the possibility of competitive edge and positioning. The theme of leadership is *anticipation*.

The focus is not on operational work but on a strategic contribution and setting and delivering a strategic intent that is often about moving to the new and shutting down parts of the old. Boundary scanning becomes important in these work levels because the strategic contribution has to do with setting the direction for the organisation and navigating it successfully through dangerous shoals.

While the added value domain looks to maximise 'what is' through continually questioning 'how', this domain is accountable for deciding on an intent that shapes the market or is appropriate to the market and then interpreting what this means to the organisation—the "why". This may be through new products, new markets, new structures, new alliances, partnerships, mergers and acquisitions, identifying new stakeholders and (where relevant) shareholders. It is certainly about image and reputation and ensuring the triple bottom line (social, economic, and environment) accountability and sustainability.

Again, there is overlap as the Innovative Domain overlaps with the Values Domain at work level V.

The Values Domain

Work in the Values Domain is concerned with creating and sustaining a shared future among multiple stakeholders often with diverse value systems within the broad socio-economic environment. Here, for example, the debate is not about winning (although certainly about group profitability and investments/disinvestments) but about agreeing to continue with the relationships despite differences.

The two work themes are Corporate Citizenship (work level VI) and Corporate Prescience (work level VII). Essentially work in the Values Domain is about managing diverse and globally distributed work level V entities. It is about creating and sustaining a shared future among these multiple stakeholders often with differing value systems within the broad socio-economic environmental context.

At the higher end of the Values Domain, the work is about judging the needs of society and deciding what types of future business is needed. Unfortunately, all too often, 'sustainability' is narrowly interpreted in terms of wealth creation from a financial capital viewpoint only. Be that as it may, even if one capital is the sole focus, the cultural and infrastructural differences are too great for any standard approach to succeed.

Organisational configurations are at minimum regionally and most likely globally. Leadership is about managing and adding value to these entities and in responding to issues threatening them. Such a global network may be comprised of tens of thousands of culturally diverse employees and include a range of business divisions, some in different industries, with many different products and brands. They will most often invest heavily in key research and development and be engaged in large long-term capital projects. Such entitles may lead or even dominate an industry and may impact across one or more industries.

Such entities wield significant power and may be concerned with shaping human values and creating contexts and institutions that in more altruistic interpretations provide steerage and stewardship around global issues of concerns but, in reality, is more often about profitability and return to shareholders.

The work at this level covers time spans as long as ten to fifty years at the absolute outside. Moving beyond the ten-year boundary in work constitutes a dramatic change as the individual now deals with multiple unified systems, overseeing, changing, buying and selling, closing down, creating new ventures, or working with large-scale system theories from the outside. This world is no longer one in which the 'future' is merely to be forecast by predicting trends or behaviours of other people or by creating multiple scenarios and watching and adjusting to that emerging future. Instead, it is a world that may be fashioned and modified despite the apparent contradictions of what is going on.

Examples of those matters which occupy these work levels may be a joint venture with significant benefits across a wide range of stakeholders, alerting and focusing on a technical breakthrough with potentially huge opportunities, the impact of a political coup on the regulatory environment, bad publicity due to a labour practice in a business subsidiary, growing extremist activities in Nigeria where the group has substantial investments, poorly performing business assets, stalled economic growth in the United States, the potential collapse of the EU, financial crises on the markets and understanding the implications of global climate change, increasing environmental constraints, disaster or mass movements aimed at specific industries, products or ways of life, and the impacts of new environmental taxes upon the cost of doing business. The executive vice-president, then, will help sustain a living context for his or her vice-presidents and take an active part in the modification and development of corporate strategy.

This is the domain of work in which the highest levels of business leadership operate, where global issues often guide economic, social, national, and hence business policy. The theme of leadership is *tolerance*.

Individual entrepreneurs who grow their vision through work level V may burst into this domain, often heralding the arrival of a new industry (or the rejuvenation of an old), complete with its own language and which in the process may reshape entire industries and social configurations. While human capability is not part of this discussion per se, one also finds individual contributors here, normally ex-CEOs, presidents, and thinkers, who in the course of their work create the context for businesses to operate globally and/or for the shift in cultural values. The power of technology and the social media has made public opinion instantly accessible, proactive, and reactive, giving wide time, greater voice, and a far sharper and more agile focus than ever before. There is also a growing involvement with issues that may shape an entirely new macro system and rewrite the rules of business in this century.

Structure of Work Level Descriptions

Each work level will be described below, broken down into the following headings to assist in understanding:

Unique purpose of the work: This describes the generic contribution that the level makes which is different from the contribution made by other levels. The generic contribution of each level is the same regardless of the business or industry.

Decision-making: The types of decisions that are made at that level of work.

Time: The length of time that is required before (a) the task completion time—the time span and which is effective for work levels I-V and (b) time to impact of decision—the time to pass before the wisdom and effectiveness of particular decisions becomes apparent. This is a key aspect for work levels VI, VII, and VIII as higher orders of complexity take longer to resolve and outcomes become more important than task completion time.

Creativity and vulnerabilities: This links to decision-making and is about the discretionary space available to incumbents at the level as well as the risks inherent in the role—what can go wrong if the person in the role is not effective.

Organisational structure: How this level of work fits into the overall organisation, and the types of structures we can expect to see around this level.

Leadership: The type of leadership that is required at this level. Note that this is not about personality type or knowledge; it is about what is required to give full effect to the unique contribution of the level so it can flow through the organisation.

Resources to be managed and performance: The resources that the incumbent at the level will be given as well as the expectations that are required to be met in order to be effective.

Case studies have been interspersed with the levels to provide practical examples of the different natures of work through the levels.

The primary case studies are as follows:

- *Executive Outcomes*—the first private military organisation led by Eeben Barlow and which heralded a change in this very old industry.
- *Virgin*—a multinational corporation led by Richard Branson which rejuvenated the service industry.
- *Grameen Bank*—a social entrepreneurial business led by Muhammad Yunus, *a new industry with its own language.*

Work Level I

Also Known as Quality

Unique Purpose of the Work

The essence of work at this level is to use skills and training to produce an output or provide a service which is largely prescribed, tangible, measurable, and meets a specific need within a specified time.

Level I, the first level of work complexity, is what is referred to as quality work or 'doing work'. Here work is about carrying out direct tasks and producing some direct output within a relatively short space of time in response to a demand.

The work can be clearly specified such as a consultant in a call centre where there are standard operating procedures and programmes that need to be marketed or issues dealt with through a set of procedures. At the high end of work level I, it may be highly skilled work such as an electrician or an artisan. At the low end, it may be completely unskilled work such a manual labourer.

There can be great variety in the tasks with levels of detail and difficulty. It may be a secretary or PA who likes to leave his desk clear at the end of each day, having worked through a defined workload with direct outputs. It may be a retail salesperson in a branch helping a customer and completing a transaction or the barista who prides herself on making the best café latte.

Work at the quality level is critical because it ensures the organisation's viability and creates value by ensuring the reputation of the organisation as a whole. It is often the first work level to have contact with the public or customer base. It is where the bottom line is met and made.

The work may be physical and often is.

Decision-Making

The incumbent needs the discretionary space to decide how to achieve the task, which is usually linked to serving the customer. This is where empowerment in work lies, and Front-Line Managers should not, unless required, transgress their limits and take away discretionary space by telling *how* the job should be done. They should set a clear purpose for the work, provide clarity about outcomes, and define what the limits of the work are. Decision-making is a direct link between action and outcome.

Time Span

Time spans may be short, failures in practical judgement and can become apparent very quickly. The period of time that is likely to elapse before the level above sees the outcome of the most complex task is half an hour to three months. People in this level do not make the final decision on setting outputs. Most issues at this level have been seen before, and if there is doubt, the matter is referred to the supervisor/team leader.

Creativity and Vulnerabilities

Significant skill, practical judgement, and knowledge are required to undertake work at this level in the modern economy. Creativity and attention needs to be paid to the variations in what is being worked on and as well as the impact of the workers decision. Thus context for the work is important as well a clear understanding. They may use judgement in dealing with non-standard issues and when referral is required.

Not only can the work be compromised if poor judgement is exercised (damaging the material, waste, incorrect solutions, lost revenue), the organisation's reputation and image to the public is often on the line. (Call centre consultant or salesperson giving wrong, misleading, or inappropriate advice, and/or unpleasant or unfriendly attitude.)

It is in the first level where productivity can be directly improved. Improvements are actively sought and indeed input is encouraged by the level above. A great deal of empowerment initiatives and programmes has been devised to do just this.

This is 'the coalface', and it is here that clients and others so often measure the organisation. Today's quality level workers are also subjected to degrees of measurement and analysis that might make even Frederick Taylor blush. It is also a level under threat as technology takes over many of the traditional hands-on, routine tasks. Creativity at this work level does not extend to making changes in schedules or programmes but is focused on the way of the individual using his/her own resources and skill to the best effect.

Organisational Structure

Work level I is the most common level of work. It provides the foundation for organisational growth and must work well, over and over again, before you can add any new work levels above it. Strategic discussions are pointless if the customer is not being attended to or the product is substandard. It is critical in almost all endeavours.

Organisational design has been impacted upon by technology and the growth in detail complexity. The old pyramid structure so often the symbol used to represent organisational hierarchy has become in some industries more of a diamond shape as unskilled workers have been shed and the bunching of work moves towards the upper limits with an ever increasing need for skills, expertise, and know-how.

Colleagues are often located together in a single site, a shop, a call centre, a construction site, a workshop, a mine, or a military unit such as a platoon.

Leadership

Leadership at this work level is the ability to organise a group of people for some purpose that produces a tangible result.

It is here where we find supervisors, and their leadership responsibility is to lead self and direct reports and to organise them for achieving a given purpose. Supervisors at this work level are supports to the Front-Line Manager. Jobholders at this level require far more intensive training and knowledge about the organisation, its products, support, and organisational information than in the industrial age. Quality workers have far higher degrees of connectivity than in the past. This is as a result of the now-not-so-new-knowledge economies.

Resources to Be Managed and Performance

This work level is responsible for achieving agreed operating cost and quality of service. It is not accountable for budgets and normally not for subordinates. However, a jobholder at this work level may direct and be assisted by a team of helpers in accomplishing a direct task.

Performance is the ability to follow instructions carefully and efficiently to solve a problem while using one's own experience and judgment to create the best outcome. Resources are those tools, instruments, and work objects required to deal directly with the task at hand.

Examples of the Work Level

This level of work is the oldest in our evolution. Before formal accountable work hierarchies existed, this work level did. Think of hunter and gatherer communities were results are immediate. The hunter would or would not have been successful in his hunt, and the women successful or not in finding and gathering the foods and delicacies.

Now jump 18,000 years into the future and think of the Medieval Craft Guilds, where specific skill and knowledge sets grew into a social and business network that was open only to the initiated. The Iron Age brought new skills into the community with early metallurgists building smelters to forge copper and later iron.

Now another jump of a mere 800 years. Work in the quality level has undergone sustained and massive change. From dangerous, repetitive factory and mining work to high-tech gleaming work spaces. The impact of technology and communications of our fossil-fuel powered society is all pervasive.

Detail complexity has mushroomed as evidenced in the growth of call centres and enabling technology that allow direct channels of sales to grow to the extent they have. Yet people continue to do work that is connected to the here and now, albeit with advanced tools and technologies (magic to our early metallurgists). Their work is aimed at meeting clients' needs and knowing how to use the sophisticated technology at their fingertips.

Training and learning are vital for performance at this level of contribution, but it is still working with direct outputs which can be measured and are defined and where the outcome can more or less be predicted with accuracy.

There is much pride in the quality level of work. Think of the small group of artisans who work in a company, making custom-made high-performance sports cars. A customer who had one of these vehicles built for him recalls being out of town the week that they were going to first start the new big 5,7 litre V8 high tech (supposedly more fuel efficient) engine. They phoned him on his mobile, excitedly asking him to listen while they turned the engine for the first time. My friend listened on his mobile, 6,000 km away as they proudly and apprehensively turned the key on the big motor. It caught instantly and settled into that deep rumble so characteristic of a V8 (a dying breed). Pride and pleasure were unmistakable emotions as the workmen said goodbye to their delighted customer.

Work Level II

Also Known as Service

Unique Purpose of the Work

This work level is concerned with the application of knowledge and experience to the particular situation or issue thereby ensuring work flow. This includes ensuring availability of resources and dealing with and resolving issues as they arise in such a manner that the image and reputation of clients and the organisations are enhanced. This would all take place within the prescribed boundaries and available resources.

Work level II is characterised by the term 'service'. Remember, each work theme is concerned with making a contribution that is different from any other work level. The contribution here is about using knowledge to provide multidirectional service, that is, to the people doing quality level I work, to customers and clients and to the organisation as a whole by ensuring their operational objectives are met.

This service can be delivered through two role types.

The first is line-management roles (Front-Line Manager), which is directed towards those direct reports at work level I, the other being individual contributors or specialists who apply a body of knowledge to solve problems for clients. They can be cross-functional or interdepartmental specialists, or they can be professionals such as doctors, lawyers, accountants, and so on.

Service may be directed to people at work level I in assisting them to organise their work, ensure that they know why they are doing the work, that they are well trained, have the right equipment, understand what they may and may not do, when to exercise their judgement, and when to call for assistance.

Front-line managers in this work ensure that the workflow is not interrupted, that working conditions are safe, and that the necessary technologies, support, budgets, and resources are available to do the job. They may solve difficult technical problems and provide the knowledge to solve and train others. This work includes forecasting demand, diagnosing problems or symptoms, and work flow. They could prepare budgets in this regard. In turn, they alert their supervisors or level III managers to trends that are unusual and suggest and receive ideas for improvement or new services.

The professionals offer specialised services to resolve and understand specific issues, often involving significant detail complexity. Knowledge may be protected to the uninitiated and/or requires special training, skills, and formal qualifications. Here professionals rely on august bodies of previously accumulated knowledge and facts to guide their exercise of judgement.

For the lawyer, it is case history and precedents and reference books on wide-ranging topics from company law, private law, criminal law, and tax laws to IP and privacy issues. For the doctor, medical procedures and medical reference books, similar symptoms and diagnosis, patient profiles; and for the accountant, general accepted accounting practices and formulas and reference books on taxes and understanding of the world of legislation and ramifications. Within an organisation, this role is often played by 'officers'—industrial relations officers, public affairs officers, tax specialists, and so on.

This diagnostic accumulation of information/data for analysis and decision-making is the same for the Front-Line Manager who, when confronted with a situation, will resort to analyse of the date to find out what has happened. This may be through talking to people, looking at data, and maybe watching video footage or listening to a recording to find out what is going on and then, based on the data, make a decision. Like the doctor, a diagnosis is made based on examination of the evidence and where necessary, conducting further investigation. Sometimes both may rely on intuition.

Decision-Making

This level of contribution is about how we use *accumulated* knowledge to make a decision. Jaques sees this as type of decision-making as one of diagnostic accumulation. Most outcomes can be visualised beforehand, but in order to do this, information must be collected and analysed in order to understand appropriate solutions.

A solution always exists and will be found. Interpretation and the use of judgement are required in understanding short-term concrete data within a framework of accredited and acknowledge know-how.

It is also about judging how best to meet a client's needs within the available resources while maintaining the image and reputation of the organisation.

People comfortable with this type of complexity enjoy evaluating options and looking for potential problems and obstacles.

Time Span

Work at this level is normally bound by the annual operations plan and budget, and the time span may range from three months up to one year. It may be from three months to as long as a year before the manager at the level above can see the conclusion of the most complex task. For example, a Front-Line Manager may decide, in response to falling customer satisfaction scores, to put their entire call centre through a particular type of training. It may be nine months before all the training is completed and the first results on customer surveys are received.

Creativity and Vulnerabilities

Creativity is to be found at all levels, but at the service levels, this is particularly important in resolving issues as it needs to take place within the frameworks and boundaries that are acceptable to the organisation, the profession, the recipient, and very often law.

No one is keen on a creative surgeon, but we may love a creative accountant. However, one needs to have the flexibility to interpret and recommend action, cope with changes in schedule, unexpected demand or downtime, and shortage of materials or staff.

The outputs of work cannot be precisely specified but is judged according to the needs of each specific situation as it presents itself and how the particular situation fits the general trends and recorded experiences. The jobholder is accountable for improving performance and meeting targets or objectives as had been agreed.

In the case of the Front-Line Manager, vulnerability at this level is being too much part of the team. For the manager at work level II, a clear understanding of their authority and accountability as discussed in Principle 5 is critical for success. Their manager is accountable for this and is part of their VARI authority and should be carried out at induction. The reason for this is that the Front-Line Manager is accountable for the collective output of the team the Mutual Knowledge Unit (MKU), which provides him or her authority to reward and initiative removal from the team. Being too much part of the team can allow personal relationships to cloud these important judgements.

Organisational Structure

It is at this work level where the mutual knowledge unit comes into existence, and one finds the first true team that has a closely shared purpose of existence through complimentary and interlocking roles.

The traditional structure of manager and direct reports is first seen at this level. There is often confusion at this level if the role of team leaders and supervisors is not clearly defined and communicated as a level I role, reporting to the Front-Line Manager the same as other staff albeit with different accountabilities.

Leadership

Leadership here is the ability to organise a group and accomplish something meaningful as required by the context of the organisation's purpose.

This work level is about leading teams or providing specialist support through non managerial roles. This is the first work level were full managers with the VARI authority of veto, assign, reward/review, and initiate removal for the role (refer Principle 5) are found. This is also the first work level were cross-functional roles (TIRR) are found.

Training can be formal or on the job, and one needs to have in place a number of competencies in order to fulfil this level of work successfully. Graduates and diplomats most often enter the world of work at this level; the very nature of graduate and post graduate study being at the minimum level II.

In the case of the professions, leadership may be an authoritative response backed by specialist knowledge and legal authority. Networks tend to be local or within a district, professional associations, or functional associations.

Resources to Be Managed and Performance

Resources are given, and this may be the employees, budgets, cost control, existing customer bases and products, manuals, suppliers, stock, systems, and technologies. The work level II jobholder must work within these constraints, provided there are no disruptions to the work system.

Knowledge is an important part of the resource of this work level and the compilation of manuals, SOPs or guidelines, and legal sign-offs by a profession may be indicative of this work level.

Work level II is about cost control, savings, operational continuity, and preparing budgets to ensure a work flow. Value is added through management of the time of operatives (direct reports, first line supervisors and contractors, and colleagues), their skills, and equipment. It is also added by effective planning of stock and anticipated needs over the next twelve months.

Performance at this work level is judged by the ability to be able solve different types of problems, given the range of potential solutions while using experience and judgement to keep the work system operating as efficiently as possible. In the case of this first level of fully authorised

Manager, their effectiveness in the above will be seen by the measureable outputs of their teams.

There are two feedback loops in work level II—firstly, one concerned with meeting the needs of internal and external clients, and secondly, ensuring that the means used achieves the required outputs within specifications (costs controlled).

Case Study

Building a Private Military Corporation[39]

The Growth of Executive Outcomes Through the Levels of Work Lens

This case study is about Executive Outcomes (EO), a Special Forces private company which redefined an industry. Eeben Barlow, founder and CEO of EO is widely regarded as the first Private Military Company (PMC).[40] EO falls under the category of being a Special Force, called in by governments and private agencies to accomplish missions that were sensitive or which could not be carried out by conventional forces.[41]

Barlow fits my definition of an entrepreneur, namely a person with an idea or an opportunity, who through taking the risk, builds an enterprise, and satisfies a real or emergent need and generates a profit or value add through these activities.

However, what makes this story also worthy of recounting is that it shaped an industry that Alvin Toffler predicted in his book The Third Wave. *Barlow created a model which would revitalise the second oldest profession in the world. Through following his working journey, we can see how different organisational levels appeared in response to a dynamic business context (Principle 1).*

Barlow's Private Military Corporation became the model for many of the large corporate structures (Blackwater Corporation and Aegis Defence Services) that have arisen in the US and elsewhere and which continue to attract attention, often criticism, censure, and sometimes legal action.

The case study starts in work level II since it often this work level where key skills are obtained and when the future entrepreneur is young. Barlow joined the South African Defence Force (SADF) at the age of eighteen with a keen desire to follow a military career. He was commissioned as an officer at nineteen with an engineering mustering.

Contextually the SADF were in the stages of entering a war in Angola. Over the ages of twenty-one to twenty-four he grounded himself in the technical skills of his trade, 'being loaned to 32 Battalion', and he became involved in Special Forces operations, primarily reconnaissance, and small team operations often operating behind enemy lines. He was accountable for achieving the mission put in front of him, utilising the resources given. This is leadership at work level II. While doing this work, he could see opportunities for improving battlefield techniques and mission planning.

(Continued in Work Level III)

Work Level III

Also Known as Practice

Manager of Managers

Unique Purpose of the Work

This work level is concerned with the coordination, integration, planning, maintenance, and management of people, technology, and resources in order to achieve specified outputs in an optimal manner.

This implies maintaining practices and systems that provide *known services and products* and variations thereon. It needs to be done in the most efficient way, thus ensuring cost containment, meeting of budgets, and ensuring that reputation and image are maintained and enhanced at the lowest possible cost. *The focus is on the known customer base.*

Here work involves identifying patterns in the actual performance of existing products or systems within an overall work system and trying to envisage the most effective and sustainable solutions to problems or opportunities. This will encompass a number of complex variables which may include people, systems, budgets, customers, time, and deliverables. The means of the organisation is created and managed.

Decision-Making

The capability of people in flow with this level of work is summarised by the term *connecting* or *serial processing*. Here, the person weighs up the current situation against that which is planned. Alternative paths are created and considered for the most favourable solution to meet future needs and ensuring continuity of workflow both present and future. These alternatives encompass implications and extrapolation and are often focused on alignment and coherence of the variables at hand as opposed to the abstract, theoretical options at more complex work levels.

Physical relocation of teams, implementing systems and processes, moving workflow from one team to another, eliminating unnecessary steps across an entire process, choosing the order of events necessary to move to a new type of production or product—these actions are examples of decisions made at this work level.

At the upper boundary of this work level, jobholders may face a dilemma. *Choices have to be made to allocate means for alternative products and services for known clients and ways of meeting the needs of those chosen clients. How far and how late do we react to developments in our environment? Here, for the first time, the requirements of the clients of the work system are not taken for granted but are related to underlying wants.*[42]

Time Span

The time span may be as long as two years before the most complex tasks can be completed and the fruits of the decision can be seen and a consistent pattern of judgement confirmed by the level-above manager. For example, the ability of a factory to regain previous production levels after a major adjustment of production processes might not be apparent until the second year under the new system. Most commonly, it is in the budgeting process for the subsequent year.

Creativity and Vulnerabilities

Creativity is twofold. Firstly, it is about improving and fine-tuning systems that are already in existence in order to operate as effectively and efficiently as possible. This implies being able to question the efficacy of the process and its systems.

Secondly, it is about managing change and developing alternative products and services and different ways of meeting the requirements and needs of known clients; in other words, taking care of the balance between ends and means.

Organisational Structure

It is at this work level that Principle 2 and specifically the MoR becomes operative for the first time. Now, a new set of specific role authority and accountabilities come into play to ensure coherence of structure, quality of leadership, review and talent identification, and management. It is this three-tier structure (the MRU) that is the basic organisational building block and has a size constraint of 300 at its maximum with 150 being optimal.

It is also here where Principle 4 becomes important, and managers need to know that one role must not report to another in the same level and that the work level is determined by Principle 3.

The Managerial Leader also needs to be able to set authority and accountabilities within his or her work structure (Principle 5). Because this is a systems approach to work, Principle 5 applies, which states that setting authority and accountability, is a cascading process so that the level IV executive must approve this structure and where required, negotiate cross-functional roles with his or her peers.

A Hinge Level

Work at this level serves as a translator role between this domain and the next. In its innovative guise, it translates new products and ideas into the operational areas of work. Can the R&D project be transferred to a commercial operation? Is it feasible from an economic perspective? Stamp[43] in her insightful manner saw validity in this distinction and dubbed the two parts of level III as *practice as continuous improvement* of *existing systems, products, and services* and the level IV component as *practice as innovation.*

The first component is continuous improvement, which is about maintaining and improving practices and systems in order that services and products to the *known customer base* is maintained and costs are contained. If possible, in such a way that reputation and organisational image is enhanced.

The second component, innovation, is undertaking projects or research work with longer time spans and which are looking at the creation of value for the future. This distinction has been most useful in recognising project work that sits at the overlap of work level III—practice and work level IV—strategic development, as *practice as innovation*.

It is of importance to recognise such work and to provide for this work level option in the organisational architecture. Project work verifies this observation as innovative projects normally fulfil the requirements of identifying new products, services, and means to serve the known and new potential customer bases, which may be internal or external.

Strategic projects are of course varied and may range from devising an action plan to deal with a proposed merger to investigating the impacts of deregulation or how to manage the talent pool of expatriates. For example, The Royal Automobile Association of South Australia (RAA) implemented a new software system that cut across functional divisions and product silos to replace a previously fragmented system. This was a full-hinge level project operating in work level IV and which required a 'rewiring' of the business. Once in place and 'bedded down', it would then become part of business as usual.

The Australian banking sector faced a dilemma as innovation and continual improvement of e-portals and alternative banking services became a drive to improve income per employee and to provide more efficient and less costly service to the client and to the banks. This was incorrectly treated as a hinge-level project and great progress was made in technical innovation but at a cost to image and reputation, which was not factored into the planning.

The efficacy of the systems alienated communities and saw the bank's image and reputations drop to an all-time low. Perceived or real declining service in city, lack of support for lower income groups and those in the bush, coupled with record profits and continued drive for greater cost efficiency has damaged what once were institutions regarded by people as the pillars of society. This complex dilemma needed to be resolved at the right work level across multiple fronts, not just the technological. However, from a project point of view, targets and objectives were accomplished in the innovative levels and bedded down into 'work as normal'.

Another example may be an innovative customer loyalty programme with time spans of up to three years and which can involve a subset of projects such as creating a single view of the customer (integrated software applications to show clients who hold multiple products in different business divisions) and loyalty and recognition schemes that have cash incentives and which are linked to credit cards and different products offered nationally.

Leadership

Leadership here is the ability to attract people consistently to new and different projects or purposes and to ensure ongoing clarity of focus, while ensuring continual improvement in daily operations.

The responsibilities of leadership at this work level are leading others who lead teams. Interactions, internally and externally, increase dramatically in numerous networks which cover different locations. There may be customer's networks, supplier networks, and peers in other departments of the organisation.

Resources to Be Managed and Performance

Resources are given. These may be IT, people, equipment, stock, machinery, premises, and vehicles. They need to be managed within the context of an integrated work system, and the key factor is control of unit costs. Financial targets and/or other targets are critically important and work holders are increasingly required to make contributions to capital expenditure plans and contribute to projected budgetary requirements.

Work level III leaders are not expected to make any decisions on the allocation of funds to meet new product developments and develop new client bases or new markets.

Adding value is achieved through effective capacity planning and resource forecasting; moving resources to meet priorities within the wider team;

benchmarking the costs of materials, services, and working methods; and being able to justify choices through cost benefit analyses. Here best practice is dictated by cost efficiency.

Performance at this work level is seen as the ability to resolve larger scale problems or those with some degree of complexity and increased variables. The ability to make choices which allow the overall system to produce more with less is a key aspect to performance at this level.

A Note on the History of the Work Level

This work level has probably been around since the time of empires, but it really came into its own with the growth of the Industrial Revolution. It became vital for production efficacy but grew to assume a new status and prestige. So grew the age of rational management. The more things could be managed and measured, the better. Pay creep, a fragmented and bureaucratic approach to work, saw *pseudo levels* emerging as non-value adding titles and pay grades proliferated.

The process reengineering movement saw the backlash with downsizing, rightsizing, and the cutting out swathes of 'non-essential' middle management. Technology produced another culling.

This overzealous application came at a cost. No work system can function effectively without this work level and attempts at giving work level II roles (reduces payroll costs) accountability and authority that span both its own work levels have failed dismally. Likewise, self-directed work teams can only succeed within a level. They cannot succeed when their activities spans processes, which cross two or more levels and hence the need for the Mutual Knowledge Unit (MKU).

Case Study Continued

Building a Private Military Corporation

The Growth of Executive Outcomes Through the Levels of Work Lens

Eeben Barlow, now a captain of specialist troops, continued to hone his skills of command as he led them on long range reconnaissance operations deep behind enemy lines. As a sapper, his own creativity came through in introducing and perfecting new combat techniques such as a technique for anti-ambush, one that would later become adopted as standard practice.

At twenty-six, he was recalled to do the prerequisite course required for the rank of major. On completion of the course, he was transferred to the Directorate Covert Intelligence (DCI), where he was sadly underutilised. Coming from the relative freedom and adrenalin rush of life in the bush to an office setting with a strict military hierarchy and protocol, no clear role, and incompetent managers; coupled with neglect and a wrong level of work; frustration and boredom were inevitable.

Like many high potential individuals (Barlow at twenty-six was comfortable with solid level III work), and who preferred asking for forgiveness than begging for permission, looked for gaps to pour his energy into and found one, carving out his own niche in DCI. This often occurs in large bureaucracies when high potential individuals are neglected or overlooked. Often they just quietly leave, but for a solider committed to a military career, leaving was not an option.

Barlow began building an effective intelligence network, not knowing how important a role it would play in his future. Another benefit that accrued during this frustrating time was experiencing his first trip abroad when he visited Turkey. The travel bug bit, and travel was to become a key part of the way the young Barlow would do business in the future.

But all was not lost at DCI. Barlow had been identified as a high-potential individual with an unusual Special Forces skill set. He was asked to join a shadowy organisation called the Civil Cooperation Bureau (CCB) as a deep cover regional commander for Europe and Asia with the rank of Colonel. The CCB has its counterparts in many countries, but it was the activities of its South African based cell and its excesses that would result in the entire CCB operation being closed down. Barlow knew none of this as he considered the offer. The CCB offer gave him the ideal opportunity to learn a new set of skills, namely business and to do what he enjoyed.

Leaving the military had not been part of his career plan, and he was concerned about having to work 'outside'. Not only would he have to survive on his own skills, he had to do his CCB work with little or no funding. Fending for oneself is a daunting task especially when not equipped with the requisite knowledge, skills, or experience and being unsure if he would value the business of business. A whole new call to adventure loomed.

(Continued in Work Level IV)

Case Study
Building a Corporation

The Growth of Virgin Through the Levels of Work Lens

Richard Branson was born on 18 July 1950. His mother, Eve, an entrepreneur wanted him to be independent and supported him in a number of unsuccessful moneymaking schemes from growing Christmas trees to breeding budgerigars. Richard had little interest in school—he failed elementary mathematics three times and university held no allure. It is reported that Richard was dyslexic, but from an early age, he could make things happen. He desperately wanted to work.

At seventeen, he started a newspaper with a friend. Richard convinced his parents to let him leave school to work full time on the newspaper. His newspaper called Student *and was launched in 1968. It is this newspaper and what he did with it that gives us our first view of his capability.* Student *was a success. The range of topics* Student *covered gives a hint of what was to come with contentious topics and interviews.*

At nineteen, he did everything himself; editor in chief, interviewer at large, production manager and advertising executive. He had no hesitation to phone and request interviews with rock stars, celebrities, and people who would one day become very famous. He asked for and received letters of support from figures such the president of the United States and Peter Sellers. He even sued the Beatles for non-delivery of a promise.

This insight into his capability shows a young man juggling a diverse range of activities that needed to be orchestrated into an outcome, namely a printed magazine. This is a good example of the serial processing ability associated with work level III capability. However, he made no money and could not produce his newspaper regularly enough. What is of special note is that some of the topics he featured in these early days would resurface thirty-five years later, as calls to action, when he transitioned into work level VII capability.

In 1969, he began his mail-order business; his first real commercial venture. Like so much to come, it was unplanned and happened because he spotted a gap in the record market. Retail price maintenance had allowed manufacturers to force shops to sell products at a minimum price, but this had been done away and none of the established businesses had wanted to enter into a retail price war. The event largely went unnoticed, except for Richard, who moved in quickly, buying excess stock from record shops. Ironically, his last edition of Student *carried his first advert for Virgin Records.*

At that stage, he had two other activities on the go as well—one was a Student Advisory Centre (SAC), a volunteer organisation set up to help answer teenage problems which continues to this day called 'Help' and the other an employment agency which sought to match underemployed nurses with London families who wanted cleaners or babysitters. More than forty years later, he would reflect that social responsibility had been important to him and cited the SAC and Student *as the start of his business ventures that had social responsibly at the core of it. We will return to this theme in the values domain.*

So here is a twenty-year-old, coordinating, managing, and driving multiple activities and even succeeding in having old restrictive legislation repealed. Richard had bigger plans in mind. He wanted to make records, not just sell them. The idea of a recording studio was on his mind . . .

(Continued in Work Level IV)

The next 'chunk' of work is the Innovative Domain of work, which concerns itself about consciously crafting the future of the company. If the first three work levels were concerned with 'how', the next two work levels are concerned with 'why.'

Work Level IV

Also Known as Strategic Development

Functional Managers

Unique Purpose of the Work

The fundamental nature of this work is to take ownership for those products/services, external and internal relationships, structures, and systems that are required for the organisation to be sustainable in changing social, economic, political, and biophysical environments.

This is true general management work and is a balancing act concerned with building the future as stated in the mission or strategic intent on the one hand, while at the same time ensuring continuation of operations. Thus the balancing act is to ensure operations continue smoothly (as represented in existing practices, structures and products) and that organisational value is maintained, that market share is maintained or grown, profit targets are met, while at the same time actively moving actively towards the implementation of the new envisaged futures.

This is the first level of contribution that seeks to make organisational impact beyond the internal focus of improving existing services.

The tricky bit is to deal with the relationship between the mission and the present and how best to get there. It is the first work level where uncertainty becomes a resource that is actively sought and used to create opportunities and space to manoeuvre. It is like having a foot in two camps; the new desired outcomes and helping to craft them and the current operational system that will need to be transformed. This may require trade-offs, but trade-offs become increasingly the nature of the game as executives learn they have far less control than did their Industrial Age counterparts.

The work is about constructing and coordinating a number of work level III tactical strategies and their processes to achieve the desired outcomes. This is where Principle 3 comes into play as a key accountability (ensuring effective work to meet the business intent).

This may be through individual contributions or steering the work of enthusiastic managerial leaders. This may also be actualised through repositioning a strategic business unit or the creation of new services/ products often via project teams (the hinge level) initially. Here (the practice/strategic development hinge level) projects are given the green light to investigate 'the new' and the feasibility to create potential value in future activities. Outcomes are evaluated to determine whether future activity is required, and if so, what should be recommended? For example, should the outcomes be embedded into the Value Added Domain and made a part of the way we do business? This decision cannot normally be made at this work level but referred to work level V.

Once agreed, the general manager or vice-president is then held accountable for the means of delivery and provide direction and steerage to the work-level III processes and practices in terms of focus and what needs to be done. This must be done while at the same managing continuity.

Thus level IV executives are the translators of the strategic intent of the organisation into what should be delivered, be it through new systems, alliances, client bases, services, or products that are necessary to achieve the intent.

Decision-Making

This work level is the first to actively use uncertainty and ambiguity as a resource. Abstract or conceptual modelling is critical for decision making and ensuring that people comfortable with this type of complex thought staff these work levels, is critical. (Principle 6 is the need to deploy people with capability to match role complexity.)

It is being able to create conceptual abstract models or pictures of how things might work, even when parts of the picture or puzzle are incomplete or unknown. Gaps in information, if not critical, are regarded as being part of the general envisaged outcome and are thus manageable.

This capability is comfortable dealing with a broad spectrum while focussing on specifics where necessary. Decisions which are made include wrestling with paradox, ambiguity, and duality of possibilities and success is determined by the ability to filter or distil through this to clarity. Capability at this level is comfortable dealing with constructing a number of parallel paths and managing the interconnections between these and synchronising them, in order to achieve the envisaged outcome.

Time Span

A time span up to five years may exist at this work level. While the definition of time span is clear, which is about time to task completion, it is important at this work level to start looking at what is the elapsed time before the outcomes of the tasks can be assessed, before the benefits or otherwise are realised. For example, the decision to shut down a particular product line may not be able to be assessed until the reactions of competitors and success of alternate product lines have all had time to cycle through.

Creativity and Vulnerabilities

Work level IV is about translating strategic intent into action. It is holding the future and translating it into what needs to be done in the present. That is why the work theme is called Strategic Development. As Gillian Stamp summarised—a general manager addresses three key questions in order to achieve this.

- *What is happening?*
- *What is not happening?*
- *What should happen?*

From the nature of these three key questions come three clearly different camps—the past, the present, and the future. The art and science lies in how best to align them. This work level of contribution is uniquely responsible for translating the strategic intent or mission of the organisation into more specific strategic business plans with the advice and input of work level III staff. These plans are normally approved at the level above or at board level.

This strategy work should not be confused with the hinge role played by work level III, where the nature of the work is project based to determine the feasibility of new products, ideas, and services.

Such plans include the creation of the detailed framework and plan for migration to the new and how best to achieve this. They normally cover a range of issues, including closing down those systems and practices that are not in alignment with the desired future; setting the framework and supplying/coordinating resources for those systems already in place, while managing the interfaces between development and current practices.

A critical part of the translating role is the assimilation of the new with established systems/practices/markets. The executive needs to be aware that there is a human cost to restructuring and reconfiguring work systems and that this cost must be monitored and damage contained.

An obvious vulnerability to this work level is the absence of or a poorly defined strategic intent (The UVA of work level V). Such absence leaves work level IV rudderless, and in such a vacuum, any course of action will do. Such situation are often played out in internal business rivalries, resulting in an organisation which may be dominated by political in-fighting, cult personalities, wasted effort, resources, and the absence of clear strategy. The consequences of decision-making or lack thereof, see loss of market share, image, reputation, and profitability.

An example of this is where the marketing communications and product offerings that should be devised at this level are not, and sales people, both in direct and indirect channels, are swamped with continually changing and conflicting offers, pricing structures, and 'new products'. In this case, the situation was compounded by a failure to apply

Principle 6 and the incumbent was overextended. Instead of working with a coherent strategy based on a long-term intent, the overextended incumbent had lowered the work level to where she was comfortable and was fighting a reactionary price strategy. This lowering of work level leads to loss of coherence, reactive marketing, conflicting advice, and work overload that training and interrelated functions cannot keep up with or comprehend.

Missing work level IV in an organisation can have serious consequences. In addressing the dilemma that the Australian banking industry fell into with its cost containment and efficiency drive, it would seem to have missed a level IV project about 'control information' associated with monitoring the added value domain of work. The risks associated with allocating large amounts of capital in new ways, products, and services (ATMS, Internet banking, telephone banking) required influencing stakeholders in a proactive way; simply reacting was insufficient.

Thus the associated campaign to make the customer base aware and the 'selling' required was not a well-conceived or orchestrated transformation plan, and this failure stung the banks longer term. It was a 'done deal' rather than the unfolding through a process of education or collaboration. The alternative more cynical and possibly pragmatic view was that the banking industry was not interested in customer response, given they were a 'captive market'.

Thus part of the control information needed at this level should come from monitoring the reactions of stakeholders. It should include the timely detection of new stakeholders.

Organisational Structure

Work level IV executives may be accountable for businesses which may have up to 2,000 employees. This is the line role (TARR) of the general manager and the organisational structure may be chunked into a number of vertical MRUs, with strong cross-functional networked role relationships. While work level IV is responsible for setting budgets, ensuring the necessary flow of resources, and the setting of and achievement of targets, it has a wide collaborative role.

External interaction is often a far more significant feature of work and may involve a far greater range of stakeholders, such as government, industry, research bodies, competitors, and strategic partners, both present and future. The nature of relationship management is increasingly proactive, as external agencies may need lobbying to change their approaches, policies, or plans, and in turn, this work level often has to anticipate changes in the operating environment which may impact on the way business is done.

Specialist work is also found at this level of contribution and is indeed a key contributor. Work may be focused on leading teams to design and develop new systems, services and products. within a particular function or advising on an aspects of the outside world—the industry, the market or a segment thereof, the regulatory conditions in a nation for example, or in providing high level specialist advice to safeguard the organisation (e.g. general manager of reinsurance) or to position it proactively in the light of real and anticipated changed conditions.

Specialist level IV work is often part of a corporate core with functional teams in different geographic locations managed through a web of TIRR roles.

Leadership

Leadership in Strategic Development is the ability to enhance a group's functioning, over an extended period of time, and its cohesion.

The responsibility of leadership at this work level is to lead multiple functions and processes. Leadership here is part of a network and best described by the term collaboration. The network extends far beyond the operating environment of the organisation or work entity and is by nature, multidisciplinary.

A clear understanding of what the strategic intent means for the division or business unit is a key component of leadership at level IV, as well as being willing to hold level III managers accountable for their own UVA and the management of their teams and undertaking the MoR accountably as they themselves are required.

Resources to Be Managed and Performance

This work level is the first to craft budgetary requirements to meet organisational strategic intent, which may require CEO and board approval for the raising of additional capital. Resources in the broader sense must be planned and negotiated based on their authoritative recommendations. Performance is measured from a strongly financial aspect but increasingly across numerous fronts, such as employees, stakeholders, customers and sustainable practices.

Here, the GM decides what to resource to the meet the new and what to terminate as well as what should continue to operate. Wide ranging technology upgrades and systems changes are approved at this level and implemented at work level III.

This may be seen in identifying major cost saving initiatives, integrating business plans, prioritising investments, and effective management of tax issues which impact on profit, creating and interpreting balance sheets, and trading statements. At the same time, this work level *must monitor* competitors' costs, quality (in relation to the competition and market), and understand the economics of the work system and its objective (for example, the value chain of supply, transport and production). Jobholders at the top boundary of the role need to ensure coherence and consistency of all the work systems in all operating units so that efficacy is maintained.

Performance at this level is the ability to resolve large scale or highly difficult problems with high quality, speed, and efficiency. This is manifested by the adaptation of the division to meet both the needs of the market and to achieve the strategic intent of the organisation.

Case Study Continued

Building a Private Military Corporation

The Growth of Executive Outcomes Through the Levels of Work Lens

Barlow, now in his undercover role, started to make his way into civilian life and into business. He realised he had to have a portfolio of activities. He became a partner in a small company while he continued to lecture at the Military Intelligence College and developed courses for Special Forces. He registered his own company, EO, as a vehicle to do the Special Forces training courses and to source covert surveillance equipment. He said 'this was an exciting and difficult time of my life' He reactivated all his agents from his time in Directorate Covert Intelligence and began to travel extensively.

But the following year his planning started to unravel as the Civil Cooperation Bureau (CCB), his employer was shut down without notice. Now unemployed and almost bankrupt, with little or no chance of recouping his disbursements from the now publically disgraced CCB, he desperately needed something else to do.

He made the decision to market EO aggressively. His reputation had grown, and he was thrilled when he was approached by a South American Drug Enforcement Agency to develop a plan to combat drugs. Barlow, in what would become his hallmark, articulated a clear and comprehensive strategy for his client with an execution plan. In other words, he offered a comprehensive work level IV response to achieve his client's intents. However, he could not be hired due to US involvement in the operation and the sanctions against South Africa. EO was also getting traction elsewhere as the fledgling company became involved with mining companies At thirty-four, he was running a number of small business units in two countries and had offices and agents in seven other countries.

During the same year, a serendipitous meeting gave Barlow the opportunity to ramp EO into a whole new level of business complexity. EO was awarded a contract to provide security for a mining company to salvage its expensive equipment of out of a rebel-held port in Angola called Soyo. Barlow hurriedly assembled a team to extract the equipment. He hoped to get in and out quickly, without alerting the UNITA rebel forces to their presence. That was not to be. Press reports alerted the rebels and brought them post-haste to Soyo. The EO Company protecting the salvage team had no option but to repulse the attacks in order to secure the mission.

He now found himself heading a small organisation that had a company of seventy-two men actively involved in combat operations who were being supplied by aircraft in continual shuttle between South Africa and Angola, a 3,000 km long logistical pipeline nightmare. From a work levels perspective EO had ratcheted from a one-man show into a fully operational 24 × 7 business that required continual resupply, logistics, intelligence, casevacs, PR, and operational planning. Barlow was busy with transport, food, medicines, recruitment, pay, training, public relations, and management of stakeholders. He was running a MRU from work level IV, and his own role was stretched thinly across all work levels. It was not sustainable.

He would later reflect that 'Soyo was pivotal to my life and the fortunes of EO'. The combat role that eventuated had not initially been planned, and the press inadvertently helped transform EO from a security/protection company into a company capable of deploying combat teams.

It was also Barlow's baptism with a different kind of fire as his efforts were greeted by a hostile press, fuelled by the South African Government, that supported the rebel movement, UNITA. This, he quickly realised, was another front that had few rules and one he was not equipped to deal with. A great deal of political pressure was being exerted, and he recognised he needed to form relationships with the media. The external world had suddenly become a whole lot more important.

The situation post Soyo grew dire as EO had no clients. This is an all too familiar entrepreneurial story. Barlow knew he had to continue marketing, but as a result of Soyo and the South African Government's response, his company was branded 'untouchable'. The stress resulted in him being briefly hospitalised for exhaustion.

But fortune favours the brave, and this situation was transformed by a surprise phone call from General Faceira Chief of the Angolan Army. He requested a meeting at which Barlow, who at the age of thirty-six, was asked to take on the role of training the Angolan Army. This time, he made certain not to repeat the mistakes of Soyo. Infrastructure was paramount, and he ensured the logistics and human resource infrastructure were in place to deal with a rapid growth in size and complexity of operations. In his clear and unambiguous manner, he drafted a strategy to help train the Angolan Army to beat the rebel forces of UNITA. This time the work levels would be in place.

In early 1994, he appointed a brigadier to command the Angolan project, which could be viewed as a work level IV strategic business unit. The Angolan Army had a very poor record of standing up to the rebels, and it was after decades of fighting, in poor health, suffering low morale, lacking equipment, and the will to win. Barlow worked on a strategy for defeating UNITA with the chief of the Angolan Army and with the Head of Intelligence. EO's Strategic Intelligence Group, which he had begun setting up as an underutilised officer in the Directorate of Covert Intelligence, ran agents in many different countries and organisations, supplying a steady stream of intelligence from different sources, agents, and combat actions.

The media war against EO continued. In trying to combat the steady and prolonged attacks on his company image, Barlow took the head of the ANC's intelligence on a tour of the Angolan operations. He regularly wrote articles and countered claims in the press.

The rebels came to the peace table as a result of the Angolan Government's success in the field and UN pressure. The talks, however, soon broke down. The Secretary General reported to UN that there was a deadlock in the negotiation process, and UNITA used the respite to rearm and commenced the offensive. This prompted the Angolan Government to escalate its plans for attack, and by mid-1994, the war in Angola reached its most crucial phase.

During April 1994, Barlow received a call from UN representative asking if EO would be able and prepared to stop the genocide in Rwanda. Barlow said he would get back in twenty-four hours, and EO presented a plan with time frame, force level, cost, deployment, and execution of the operation. The UN response was that it was too expensive. Three months later, more than one million people had died.

Barlow met with Paul Kagame in 1995 to discuss the situation. He outlined to Kagame how EO would deal with the Rwanda issue, offering a clearly defined strategic intent and the 'business plan' to achieve the desired outcome. But it was too late. Barlow was of the view that no one in the international community cared what happened in Rwanda, since there was neither oil nor diamonds, except, he said, with prescience, water, and one day the world will go to war for that. Barlow felt most African conflicts were a play for natural resources.

EO has become known for offering clients a clear and cohesive strategy in all their contracts with costs and timelines. The company was building a reputation for being able to deliver in volatile and hostile situations through articulating clear strategies and delivering on them. This could not be done from any other work level than IV with a CEO who had a clear understanding of the issues at the next work level . . .

(Continued in Work Level V)

Case Study Continued
Building a Corporation

The Growth of Virgin Through the Levels of Work Lens

Entrepreneurs normally carry at least three levels of work in their mind simultaneously. They contribute (and often get in the way of others) for at least two and think about the third—the more complex and yet-to-emerge work level.

At twenty-one, Branson already had created a portfolio of business activities. His mail-order business had given him the idea of becoming further involved in the music industry. He told his cousin, Simon Draper, that he planned a full-fledged music empire, including a chain of recording studios, a management company, a music publishing business, and a record label (logo designed). Branson said to Simon Draper, who had a deep knowledge of music, 'You can start my label.'

So here was his dream—a vision—of what he wanted his business to look like in the future. Just like Bill Gates, who had envisioned people using his software on PCs before PCs were invented, Branson also had a vision. In order to further his plan, he purchased the Manor, at the cost of £30,000, ending up with a mortgage of £22,500. This is a clear example—like Gates—of a young man holding a conceptual multifaceted mental model of what he wanted his business to look like and was working towards achieving that vision. This is a clear example of emerging thinking at work level IV.

In the process of importing music, he had a brush with the law, and it gave him a salutary lesson on how to conduct his business. The outcome was owing HM Customs and Excise a significant amount of money but at least he avoided jail. He had to pay an immediate down payment of £15,000 and £38,000 over three years. This was a daunting amount for Virgin at that time and for a young man of twenty-one with a new mortgage. It has been suggested that this was added incentive for his business growth. The great coup of its early years was signing up Mike Oldfield and Tubular Bells. In 1973, Tubular Bells allowed money to flow into the company coffers.

But Branson was still on the prowl. From the seventies onwards, he focused on getting international foreign distribution rights for Virgin since it allowed for more profit. He also still wanted to be a newspaper owner as he retained a fascination with a product having a short time span and wanted the respectability that came with the role and ownership. He had a disastrous attempt at establishing a magazine, but its failure did not deter him. He already had a publishing house bought in 1979 called Virgin Books, but it was not doing well.

A foray into film-making cost dearly and taught him a valuable lesson about being at arm's length in negotiation and not to be dazzled by the glamour of a movie business. In 1978, the twenty-eight-year-old Branson bought a private island for £300,000 and two nightclubs for a million pounds.

(Continued in Work Level V)

Work Level V

Also Known as Strategic Intent

Business manager/CEO/MD

Unique Purpose of the Work

The essence of work at level V is the formulation of an organisational Strategic Intent—which is the articulation of a desired and achievable future position. This intent provides direction and coherence to that organisation or division in order to deliver its desired outcomes. It is also accountable for ensuring in collaboration with the level above or the board; organisational viability.

The essence of this work is about agreeing on and guiding the organisation along a path towards desired scenarios and outcomes. Jaques refers to this level of work as the most interesting since it is where unified whole systems are created. Principles 1 and 2 are relevant here since this is where the complexity of the operation dictates that it is indeed a five-level work structure that is required, and this is determined by the application of Principle 1 (UVA) and Principle 3,(time span).

Unified systems require frameworks to operate coherently. The frameworks created at this work level bind the organisation as an entity and as a system that is intact yet operating in an open environment with clear purposes in mind (the intent). The framework is multifaceted. One of the unique value adds at this work level is *creating these frameworks.*

They are necessary for enforcing financial control and governance, for setting overall direction of business targets and objectives, for the raising of investment capital, for ensuring image and reputation, and for setting guidelines in seeking alliances and partnerships and in making investment decisions.

The Strategic Intent defines much of the accompanying frameworks, and within it are encapsulated multiple strategies across a broad front to address the progression of the entity. Here for the first time, the external environment impacts directly on the entity, providing directives and imperatives that drive many aspects of the frameworks. These may be the requirements of the Financial Services Act, regulatory requirements, tax, employment, and a host of other legal and governance needs.

There is a number of diverse unique value adds (UVAs) in this role. This includes managing the organisation as a social being: its employees, partners, suppliers, shareholders, and the broader stakeholders within which it is embedded and within which its client bases are found. Work at this level may be seen as managing what Brian Dive[44] describes 'as resource boundaries, identifiable as complete entities'. Roles at this level may be those of a managing director, a chief executive, a member of an executive group of a large complex corporation that is national or multinational. The role may also be of a specialist contributor or being accountable for a global income stream or discipline.

Another key UVA is that of innovation—deciding on new products, new markets, new ventures or alliances. Poor judgment at this level can impact on a company's image, reputation and sustainability. Here one needs to balance short profits with longer term strategies for growth and profitability.

Decision-Making

Principle 6 states match individual capability to role complexity. Individuals appointed in this level of work must *have the current actual capability at that given point in time to carry out the level of work complexity required.* This means stepping out of one's own functional area and having to value multiple functional areas equally. It is no longer enough to be 'a marketing person' or a 'CFO.'

The abstract and conceptual analysis of work level IV now changes to holding the multiple mental models required to lead a number of whole systems operating within the frameworks that we have discussed above.

Competition for resources, time, and personal attention are demanded. The ability to process and filter out noise and important information is critical. Stamp talks here about the ability *to weave* information and to see the links between bodies of knowledge, information, products, and clients as being clues to innovation and positioning.

Uncertainty and ambiguity are key parts of the process of problem solving. Leaving situations open and fluid does not produce results, although often this is the modus operandi that individuals at this level may use before making the critical decisions. The ability to drive out uncertainty in creating operating frameworks is the gift of problem solving at this work level. Work level is a fractal of work levels I and III.

Jaques regards this cognitive shift into work level V challenges as a major change because it sees individuals moving from the 3rd Order of Information Processing (conceptual abstract) to worldwide *declarative processing*—the 4th Order of Information Processing.

Performance at this work level is the ability to resolve large scale or highly difficult problems with high quality, speed, and efficiency.

Time Span

At this level, the rules of the game for the next decade are consciously made, and this is the highest level of an organisation where decisions and choices made are aimed at implementation in the operational domain of work.

It is thus the highest executive level. Innovation and changes made at this level always imply many work systems, and the emphasis is on the redesign of relations between these work systems.

The time span for decision-making becomes critical at this level. CEOs are both seduced and hamstrung by short-sighted markets and the promise of their stock-linked remuneration packages. The success of CEOs is often judged on the share price when they leave the organisation, and to the chagrin of the public, they are often rewarded when they fail dismally in their long-term obligations.

The vulnerability is that immediate results are not available to verify the choices they make. *The more complex decisions create a point of no return which starts a new organisational growth curve*. Thus the choices made at this level can result in beneficiaries and victims among the stakeholders, and who is what is not always clear until the passage of time. By then, the CEO is normally long gone. So often it is more useful for boards to talk about consequences of decision as a measure of complexity and the work level.

The consequences of decision-making of the most complex decisions made by a CEO during his or her tenure may be measured by the shareholders over a time frame of five to an upper limit of ten years. Five to seven years is more common. However, short term consequences of failing to exercise judgement or being mindful of decisions made at lower work levesl, are not to be ignored as the forced exit of the CEO and Chairman of Barclays Bank in 2012 testified[45].

Creativity and Vulnerabilities

Work level V offers a dual perspective; *outward to ensure long-term viability and at the same time inward, to create and sustain optimal-working conditions*.

The building of a strong internal culture, image, and reputation is a critical at this level. The value of aligning people with a challenging, interesting, and compelling organisational vision cannot and should never be understated.

People need to feel they are part of something great, something special that they are able to contribute and that their contribution means something. It is the unique value adds of this role, and it is to ensure that people are aligned and motivated by the vision of the company.

There is the need to ensure that actions are congruent with values, and the CEO and his management team must reinforce vision, with the *CEO, at all times, acting as the organisations role model—its exemplar*. There are high demands on the time of the CEO, and it is very difficult to balance these needs while giving out the same coherent message on all fronts. Thus high degrees of consistency, presence, and alignment need to be carried out, specifically by work level IV executive management. These are the translators par excellence. This alignment and coherence and vision for how everyone can contribute reflect back to the communities that are served at level I and in the operational domain at large.

This work level is the highest part of a complex independent company or subsidiary operation. A CEO who is responsible for both direction (guiding the organisation through its interactions and impact with stakeholders and the economic, political, and social environments) and sustainability (signalling its reputation, image to existing, new, and potential stakeholders in the external world that it is viable, competitive, and a long-term player) is operating in the Values Domain as well as in the Innovative Domain.[46]

In a company situated in the Innovative Domain, such as a subsidiary, this responsibility may be split between the CEO and the board, with the board concerning itself with viability issues and the CEO with direction.

Organisational Structure

Achieving the Strategic Intent is like navigating the entity on the ocean of the world. This is open active navigation requiring constant vigilance to note shifting sandbanks, changed navigational beacons, traffic, weather forecasts, navigational notices, prevailing wind, current, fuel, victuals, morale, safety, ensuring maintenance of equipment and propulsion systems, while reassuring stakeholders that their cargo is in safe hands, and continually updating the ETA. The captain of this ship must, while doing all this, maintain the ability to change course or take appropriate action to accommodate and take advantage of anticipated or real changes in the environment.

This may mean, in the business sense, reconfiguration of the organisation by closing down divisions/business units/functions, creating new entities, or amalgamating existing entities to maintain an optimal course in order to achieve the strategic intent. Here decision-making in terms of investments, new technologies, and new alliances may carry significant consequences if poor judgement is exercised or due diligence is not carried out.

The entities being shaped are now complex social institutions, businesses, public or private, general theories, and concepts rather than material things or discreet programmes and systems. The individual operates a complex whole system and is able to modify the boundaries of that system. An example would be the CEO of a subsidiary of a large corporation whose role is to shape and reshape the business he or she controls. He or she may push out its boundaries in one place into new market opportunities or a bold new technology or joint venture.

But this brings trade-offs, and she or he will have to make the necessary consequential adjustments, for example, pulling in its market boundaries elsewhere or withdrawing marginal production runs or a product line.

For entrepreneurs, development of their business into this work level may take decades, bearing in mind that most companies have a lifetime of twelve years and level V structures, about forty years. For those entrepreneurs, who do grow work level V organisations, unless they meet Principle 6, they lose control of their organisation to JVs or acquisitions as more capable leadership takes control of the bigger entity. The story of Microsoft and Virgin are rarities as their founders had the cognitive capability and nous to grow the company through successive levels of work complexity to work level V and outmanoeuvre the competition. Time will tell which of them, including the new giants of Google and Facebook will survive the forty-year average.

Leadership, Skills, and Competencies

Leadership here is the ability to exercise a catalysing effect on many different groups, irrespective of being internal or external to the organisation, competitor, or strategic partner.

Leadership at this work level is about leading business *and delivering agreed outcomes.* It requires the ability to galvanise many diverse and large groups. At a corporate level ability, leadership may be measured by the ability to accomplish very difficult or very large-scale changes or both.

Jim Collins, co-author of *Successful Habits of Visionary Companies,* in his article 'Level 5 Leadership'[47] detailing in a research project which began in 1996, found that executives at companies that went from good to great, sustained that performance for fifteen years or more. All had a level 5 leadership in place at the time of the transition. Furthermore, the researchers found that absence of level 5 leadership showed up consistently amongst other less successful organisations. 'Level 5 is an empirical finding not an ideological one.'

Collin's level 5 leadership hierarchy is a mixture of the levels described here plus personal attributes. His first 4 levels are indeed similar, while 5 is not a description of work complexity but individual capability and other attributes. However, in essence, the concept of levels of distinct complexity and leadership requirements is once again confirmed.

Principle 7 is of importance to the CEO or MD for ensuring that a coherent language and understanding of managerial leadership practices is in place and that this is adhered to. This is one way of strongly influencing culture, and this should be system supported. Managerial Leadership competence is not a luxury, it is critical to high performance. It requires a common effective daily language and common sense practices that are clearly understood and used in everyday life at all work levels.

Resources to Be Managed and Performance

The role of executives at this level includes *securing investment capital, active and consistent tending to image, reputation, and financial issues for creating confidence in the complex web of relationship within which the business is hosted.*

This is the business and its employees, the investor community, shareholders, and all its stakeholders. The CEO needs to convince these often disparate and conflicting audiences that the company is being managed and led to ensure sustainability and viability over the longer haul.

The role of a work level V managerial leader is far more externally focussed than at work level IV. Players need to be alert to developments which he or she may detect or which are signalled to them and which may come from sources internally or externally. These represent opportunities or potential threats.

Roles at this level, which are responsible for specialist work, such as the Chief Scientists at the CSIRO, should be focussed on the creation of new knowledge. Here the outputs are not expected to have short-term application but may be expected to add value within longer time scales which may extend up to the ten-year boundary. This is not to say such roles do not carry business or commercial responsibilities; they may well do so, and this fact does create tensions for the organisation as well as the CEO.

Performance at this work level is the ability to resolve nearly any problem, repeatedly, with best in class levels of performance.

The twenty-first century is pushing for social accountability, environmental sustainability, and tighter financial constraints—the triple bottom line is making real impact with legislated requirements. No organisation is safe from the consequences of decision-making that is based on financial factors only. Activists target brands and how an organisation or division or group is perceived 'out there' hits the bottom line. It is no longer sufficient to woo shareholders only with share prices or dividends or for the sales division to woo customers through unethical practices and misleading information, as the multi billion dollar fines to GlaxoSmithKline testify[48] In this case activities of staff in the Value Added Domain impacted negatively on image and reputation at the group executive levels. Community anger and disenchantment may erode reputation, image, and profits over the longer term. Thus, while level V is responsible for returns on financial and human capitals, it ignores reputation and image at its peril. Market position and economic value added are far more complex-networked issues. Sustainability has quietly evolved to take on a whole new meaning.

Case Study Continued
Building a Private Military Corporation

The Growth of Executive Outcomes Through the Levels of Work Lens

Sierra Leone

As 1994 dawned on the world, EO continued its operations in restoring Angola to its elected government and bringing a closure to one of the longest civil wars. Meanwhile, the small country of Sierra Leone was in turmoil, a microcosm of the breakdown of law and order that was occurring in West Africa. The international community had no desire to become embroiled, and the UN was dealing with the aftermath of seeing dead American soldiers being dragged through the streets of Mogadishu and other incidents in Bosnia and Rwanda in which the UN peacekeepers had publically failed.

Tony Buckingham, CEO of Heritage Oil, who had given Barlow the original Soyo contract, contacted him again, asking if EO was willing to go to Sierra Leone to assist the president, no blushing violet himself, who had taken power through a coup. Barlow was told of the enveloping chaos, and he agreed to talks with the Sierra Leone president. The UN, not surprisingly, was suspicious of the president but stood by watching as the anarchy unfolded. Sierra Leone had tensions with its neighbours who were aiding and abetting the RUF rebel forces.

Diamonds and mining issues were at the heart of the internal conflict as the diamond fields allowed them to fund their activities and buy arms and support neighbouring regimes. Liberia and its strongman leader Charles Taylor, were aiding and abetting the RUF and was growing rich out of the RUFs control of the diamond fields.[49]

Barlow, after his talks, could see a plan coming together but one which was geared around flexibility as EO had very little information to work with on arrival. Once a contract was signed, an advance party quickly established itself with the purpose of obtaining effective intelligence. A state-of-the-art communications net soon provided much-needed intelligence, and the campaign moved ahead. It was a small force seldom over 250 men using second-rate equipment and one helicopter gunship.

They launched aggressive combat patrols and hunted the rebels, taking the diamond fields in record time thus denying the rebels funding.

EO's involvement was from 25 May 1995 until March 1997. Shortly after EO left, the UN's promised peacekeeping force did not materialise, its members baulking at the cost and a coup brought the RUF back from the brink of defeat and in an alliance with a new military Junta into power. Sierra Leone fell apart with great bloodshed and savagery. After bitter fighting and the intervention of the British, order was restored.

In 2003, a democratically elected President Kambah would say how his hand had been forced to terminate EO's contact in spite of popular opposition. Huge loss of life and heavy financial consequences followed the premature termination of that contact.

Elizabeth Rubin in a New York Times *article on 4 February 1999 wrote a piece titled* 'Saving Sierra Leone' *and in this she said,* 'The company was willing to do what the UN cannot—take sides, take casualties, deploy overwhelming force, and fire pre-emptively. EO agreed to put down the rebels and restore law and order in return for $15 million and diamond-mining concessions. Relying on about two hundred soldiers and a helicopter gunship, it nearly succeeded. Three hundred thousand refugees were able to return from squalid camps in neighbouring Guinea that were costing the international community $60 million a year. And within a year, the people of Sierra Leone voted in their first presidential election in twenty-eight years.'

The tumultuous ten-year cycle finally ended in June 1997 when Barlow resigned from EO. He cites a host of reasons—disagreement, greed, meeting his personal objective, and after giving his shareholding to his men, he walked away, believing the company to be in good health. He felt he had achieved what he had started and was tired. He wanted to do something else with his life.

People with capability to enter into and work through work level V in their forties (meaning their Growth Mode will take them strongly into the Values Domain of Work) often creating innovations that become legacy. There is no doubt that Barlow's EO left a legacy that is being played out today through many other PMCs.

For each project, Barlow articulated a strategic intent with a master strategy for success before the contracts were signed. This included careful execution of the strategy. Strategy formulation is a key competence of all executives in work level IV and above. The Principles and the sequence of events determine that the creation of structure follows strategy, and from strategy, the nature of the work can be deduced and roles defined. The right people are found and deployed; empowered to exercise judgment within the terms of the intent and developed in Managerial Leadership competence.

Barlow authorised his officers to carry out their accountabilities with very little, if any apparent interference once a strategy was agreed. Like with any complex system, he only interfered if serious disagreements on strategy arose or relations at the level above needed attention. As CEO, he was focussed on adding his unique value without interfering with his team, who he felt were capable, committed and had agreed to follow the approved strategy or course of action.

EO was involved in two theatres of operations both conducted by MRU structures (the three-tier building blocks) of optimal size. However, being 'standalone' units, where their commanding officers (appointed as brigadiers) had to deal with higher level of works (political, social, and commercial) they were led at work level IV.

Barlow's own UVA was sourcing work and dealing with stakeholders in level V and above while providing strategic campaigns plans for execution in work level IV.

(End of case study)

Case Study Continued
Building a Corporation

The Growth of Virgin Through the Levels of Work Lens

By the age of thirty-one, a decade after he had closed down Student *to concentrate on selling records by mail order Branson's work had shifted significantly. He had established a patchwork of interrelated businesses ranging from work level I to IV. That included a record label, a studio business, a chain of shops, and music publishing house. He had achieved his vision of a decade earlier.*

His unique value add as CEO was continual boundary scanning, spotting gaps in the market for new or revitalised products and services, new markets, innovative means and methods, and new and existing customer bases with better offering. The important thing to grasp here is that he was not just focussed in one industry or on one business. He was doing this type of assimilating, processing, and scanning across multiple businesses and industries.

By the mid-1980s, Branson had withdrawn from daily control over the record company. One can image the sigh of relief he must have given when he could gratefully let go of the work level II elements '. . . thankfully, Branson was no longer responsible for climbing aboard an aircraft with a suitcase full of cassettes and carrying it exhaustedly from one office block to the other, trying to sell the work of Virgin artists in Britain for distribution in the United States'.[50]

He had instinctively created an organisation where authority and accountability was clearly delegated. In fact, one of his strengths is his ability to empower role relationships (Principle 5) and creating businesses of optimal size (Principle 3). Since 1978, he had not been involved in management decisions. This behaviour seems to be that of someone comfortable with the complexity of a work level V role. Even the overseas distribution deals were now left to his direct reports.

From a requisite managerial perspective, he had delegated authority and accountability to competent people, empowered to further the success of the business. He would only go back to those work levels if they were failing. An example of this emerged is that during the course of 1984, the marketing director of Virgin Atlantic kept being undermined or interfered with by Richard Branson, who gave his managers lots of space when a business was stable and running successfully and would not hesitate to step back in and disrupt the chain of command when there was uncertainty and failure. Like other complex adaptive systems, the next level will only subsume responsibilities of the level below when that level is not working optimally or is under threat. Remember that the level above is there to create optimal conditions for the immediate level below.

His passion for his staff is well known. What it did was to ensure through feedback loops that the link between quality and service and practice as innovation was closely tied to image and reputation of Virgin. As Virgin expanded, this would become very important.

But all was about to change as he grew more firmly into work level V capability. This is for many high-mode entrepreneurs and thought leaders, the work level where it often all comes together. Work level V is where established industries can be reshaped, restructured, and turned on their heads. It is where industry leadership is forged. It is also where new industries with a new language can be created. This is the work level where Muhammad Yunus set up microcredit as a new industry; where James Lovelock formulated the Gaia hypothesis; on the other side of the spectrum, where Eeben Barlow set a global precedent for new Private Military Corporations; and where Zuckerberg works to create 'an open world'. People who can shape at this work level often find or settle into their true purpose.

The Virgin Group was a jumble of piecemeal businesses, which was in May 1984, moving towards a £100 million turnover but with little profit. The record side of Virgin was doing fantastically, but the rest of the group was a collection of different businesses with no management structure, no information systems, a bank, and set of advisors that did not meet its needs. The company was struggling to expand without working capital and had an inadequate overdraft. This was without taking into account that Branson wanted to launch an airline, and which as we all know, he did.

At the end of 1985, with the New York route stabilised, Branson was ready to start thinking about acquiring a second aircraft and opening up a second destination. By 1986, his role had developed into a full work level V role with a strong external focus. He was active in lobbying ministers about issues that concerned his industries where he was active (e.g. airline protection, copyrights, and legislation), and he had become used to invites from government officials. He was on good terms with the prime minister and had become involved with some government initiatives.

Branson then turned his attention to another project, namely condoms, where a monopoly held sway with uncompetitive practices. He managed to source condoms at a drastically reduced rat and, set up a new venture and brand with a new CEO—created vending machines in 18,000 in pubs and garage outlets across the country, dwarfing the opposition's 2,000 outlets. This was very successful, and the company, Healthcare, was profitable within a year. He reduced the price of condoms, and £1 million in profit was given to charity organisations. The brand was later sold. This foray into condoms was well timed as AIDS was spreading like wildfire. It would be a social-responsibility theme he would return to many years later in a different work level with a nation-building intent.

By 1990, he had doubled the size of the airline, and Virgin was now a multinational company. One of the major vulnerabilities of a CEO in a full-fledged level V business is the balance between internal and external focus. Some CEOs are all out there, with the result employees, internal systems and leadership issues are neglected while others are all in there without paying sufficient attention to the external environment and the need for continual boundary scanning. Richard seems to have balanced this well as employees were his no 1 focus, placing them before customers. He brought a certain kind of magic and great service to his customers and was the source of many innovations, including the personal video screens in every seat back.

He learnt a sharp lesson in the property and development market, losing a good deal of money, swept away by thinking he could make easy and swift returns on a market boom of the late eighties. The moral of lesson he learnt was to stick close to businesses that produced services or delivered goods that consumers wanted, and this refocused his strategic intent and where he wanted his organisation to be able to add value.

(Continued in Work Level VI)

Case Study
Building a Social Entrepreneurial Business

The Growth of the Grameen Bank Through the Levels of Work Lens

Muhammad Yunus, founder of the Grameen Bank and the microfinance industry, is a visionary.[51] *In 2006, he was awarded the Noble Prize for his work in empowering people through microcredit. Muhammad Yunus stood banking on its head by choosing a model that was in many ways the antithesis of globally accepted practices. Over time, his experimentations reversed conventional banking practice by removing the need for collateral and bringing back human traits like mutual trust, accountability, participation, and creativity. His remarkable journey built up an institution that empowered and liberated the poor and which has been replicated around the world.*

Traditional banking benefits those who already have wealth in some form or another, and to borrow money, you need to put up collateral. The banking system is built on distrust and not trust. The preference is for lending large amounts to a few clients and contact is limited to annual reviews, debt servicing, or marketing. Fighting poverty is not part of traditional banking's mission.

The young Muhammad finished school in sixteenth position out of 39,000 students. After completing a BA and a MA in economics at Dhaka University, he joined the Bureau of Economics in 1961 where he worked as a research assistant. At twenty-one, he decided to try his hand at business, setting up a packing-and-printing plant. This was the first company of its type, and it quickly became profitable and employed more than a 100 workers. This gave him confidence that he could earn his own money, but teaching was his true love, and he continued, while being a businessman, to teach. In 1965, the twenty-five-year-old received a Fulbright Scholarship, departing for the US to do a Ph.D. in economics.

In 1971, the War of Liberation broke out as the new Bangladesh emerged. He returned to Bangladesh in 1972, full of idealism and burning to work towards a new future. The new government snapped up the economics Ph.D. graduate, but he soon resigned, feeling underutilised and not being able to make a contribution. The thirty-two-year-old took up the post as head of economics at Chittagong University where not so long ago, he had studied and taught. What he did not know then was how its neighbouring village, Jobra, would become a fertile breeding ground for his ideas. His apprenticeship in life would soon start.

In 1974, the Bangladesh famine became acute. It is estimated that over a million people died in the Bangladesh famine of 1974-1975. The causes are generally attributed to a combination of natural disasters, in the early 1970s, and socio-political factors that followed the Bangladesh Liberation

War. Yunus felt useless, asking himself how could people suffer like this. Starving people flocked to the city in search of food, and the dead and dying were all around. He approached the head of the university, a respected national leader, to sign a petition to urge the government to act. All the teachers signed it as well. Yunus watched in horror and alarm as the famine intensified. What else could he do? He wanted to help the poor but how? He could see that the current way of doing things was not working.

He started questioning what he taught—the elegant theories and models, the vast sums of money, and the whole knowledge base that supported it. The more he thought about this, the more it fell short of the mark, and, worse than that, it was failing humanity. Here people were starving, yet the world was awash with capital and resources to halt the process. He decided to redefine his role and how he might be able to help. Where to start?

He realised how small amounts of money made a difference between life and death and between economic slavery and hope and empowerment. At one point, early on, he lent a group of people $27 to help them break the vicious cycle of poverty and money lenders. As he explored the village, he started to unlearn his economic theory about how things should work and began to learn from the real world and specifically how economics really worked. At thirty-four, he realised that he needed an institutional solution.

Ignoring his social standing as a professor, he was out and about in the village, on the farms, and working in the fields. He saw firsthand how lack of knowledge about local conditions, poor planning, and lack of funding resulted in lands standing devoid of water while expensive Tubewell irrigation systems, installed by an international development project, stood around unused. He introduced what was called a 3 Share Farm Experiments, a sharing arrangement between farmers, sharecropper, and the university. He was trying to bring academia, development aid, and the village together.

He saw the failure of development projects, how the cycle worked, where development money flowed between agencies to government and into the hands of the already wealthy and to consultants and a host of service and support companies. He saw how these huge projects failed to impact or uplift the lives of the poor. Development projects of schools, highways, government buildings, and other 'prestige projects' failed to trickle down to where jobs, money, and real development could take place.

But Yunus was not discouraged. He was overwhelmed with human ingenuity in the face of survival. His focus was on the poorest of the poor. His experiments confirmed that a small amount of money provided a ticket to self-discovery, growth, and personal development that could impact far beyond the individual. It offered the key to solving poverty and turning lives around.

Over a period of time, he and his students devised a scheme whereby they targeted women as borrowers. Women, in many traditional societies, are marginalised with few rights. So was it in villages and towns in Bangladesh, like Jobra. It was difficult work getting access to them and winning their trust because the culture and society had erected so many barriers. However, Yunus and his students formed them into borrower groups and offered support and process. He realised that borrowers needed to belong to a group, and group membership was critical for support and purpose. First daily and then weekly loan repayments were instituted. Progress was slow as work level I (deciding on the loans according to guidelines) and II (the process and resources availability) was slowly built.

As mentioned earlier, entrepreneurs normally carry up to and work with three work levels as they build their enterprises. While level I and II processes, procedures, and efficiencies were being experimented with, Yunus was busy working across work levels II, III, and IV.

When trying to access funding, he ran into a brick wall with the traditional banks. The poor were regarded as un-bankable, and the leading national bank would not consider partnering him in such a risky venture. The best they would do would lend him a maximum of $300 in his personal capacity. This led to a paper chase of him having to approve each loan with the paperwork following him around the country and abroad. He needed to find a work level III systems solution to handle funding, loans, and repayments that would also build a sense of community among borrowers.

In 1976, he secured a loan with the Janata Bank, but his view of how loans should work clashed fundamentally with the traditional banker's view of credit and collateral, and he was outspoken in his condemnation of this. Yunus wanted a people-worthy bank and one build on trust with close contact between the borrowers and the lenders and small regular repayments. He said he looked at what other banks did and then did the opposite.

In 1977, he started the first year of the banking experiment, and during that year, he had an opportunity to form an alliance with the Agricultural Bank and establish a full-fledged independent branch. This joint venture provided him with a flexible solution—a work level IV solution—to his practical need for a system.

Armed with a kitty of one million taka, he was able to frame rules and policies, select staff, and get on with it for an uninterrupted year before doing a review to see how the experiment had gone. Progress was faster than with the Janata bank, but they still had less than 500 borrowers. In 1978, Yunus won the President's Award for the work with the 3 Share Experiment, but he was still unhappy. He needed to differentiate the really poor. What concerned him were the women he had seen fighting over obtaining back-breaking work in the project and how the project had not benefited them at all.

The Grameen project got its break in 1978 when he formed an alliance with the Central Bank which allowed for greatly expanded operations so that by 1979, he had a total of 19 branches. Yunus took leave of absence from the university and joined the project full time. The year 1981 was a key time as it marked the end of the two-year experiment. The MDs of the Central Bank agreed it had been a success but said that it was based on Yunus himself, and there could not be a Yunus in every branch.

Yunus becoming very angry at this because they had not understood he had set up a new banking structure that did not require his presence at all! By 1982, they had grown to 28,000 borrowers from less than 500 in 1979. He had now consolidated a work level IV organisation led from work level V with a market, product, infrastructure, and governance. The branches were MRUs and the lending circles, were in effect, MKUs.

He offered the Central Bank's MD's a challenge, saying he would spread the experiment over a much larger area in a five-year expansion plan and would find an international donor to support the operations. The Ford

Foundation agreed to put up US$800 million in reserve, and by the end of 1981, they had US$13.4 m in loans.

In 1982, Muhammad's dream was realised when the Bangladeshi president made it a separate banking institution, and at the age of forty-three, the Grameen Bank was born. Over the next few years, structural adjustments to shareholding and board appointments took place, giving the Grameen Bank its independence and had become a full-fledged work level V structure.

In his own words, 'In creating Grameen Bank, I never had a blueprint to follow. I moved one step at a time, always thinking this step will be my last step. But it was not. That one step led me to another step, a step which looked so interesting that it was difficult to walk away from. I faced this situation at every turn.

'I started my work by giving small amount of money to a few poor people without any collateral. Then I realised how good the people felt about it. I needed more money to expand the programme. To access bank money, I offered myself as a guarantor. To get support from another bank, I converted my project as the bank's project. Later, I turned it into a central bank project. Over time, I saw that the best strategy would be to create an independent bank to do the work that we do. So we did.

'We converted the project into a formal bank, borrowing money from the central bank to lend money to the borrowers. Since donors became interested in our work and wanted to support us, we borrowed and received grants from international donors. At one stage, we decided to be self-reliant. This led us to focus on generating money internally by collecting deposits. Now Grameen Bank has more money in deposits than it lends out to borrowers. It lends out half a billion dollars a year, in loans averaging under $ 200, to 4.5 million borrowers, without collateral and maintains 99 per cent repayment record.

'We introduced many programmes in the bank—housing loans, student loans, pension funds, loans to purchase mobile phones to become the village telephone ladies, loans to beggars to become door-to-door salesman. One came after another.'[52] (Muhammad Yunus)[53]

(Continued in Work Level VI)

The next 'chunk' of work is the Values Domain, and here work is about consolidating and growing a global position and ensuring resources and assets to sustain them as an entity.

While work level V CEOs are focussed on wealth creation for a unified work system, executives in the next two work levels are focussed not only enhancing the value of a number of such entities globally, they search and fund new developments.

This domain has in recent years seen spectacular business failures caused by the GFC. Time spans of decision-making driven by short termism and greed and now aided by instantaneous communication and technology has seen poor judgement passed along entire value chains.

This domain of work is under threat across multiple fronts.

It is the domain of work in which the highest levels of global business and government leadership operate. Increasingly environmental issues are limiting the freedom to pursue economic, social, national and business objectives.

As a result of the confluence of many factors, we are in the midst of seeing an entire new work level emerge.

Work Level VI

Also Known as Corporate Citizenship

Group Executive

Unique Purpose of the Work

Work at this level is concerned about the leadership, coordination, and integration of a network of separate companies, divisions, or strategic business units. It is about monitoring and enforcing connectivity between these entities and the group and the different contexts within which they operate. The actions of a business unit impact the larger corporation in many ways, and when this is negative, the whole brand, or corporation may suffer, such as not planning effectively for stakeholder's responses or environmental pollution. News Corp is one example of the former, BP of the latter.

Thus creating a 'friendly world' is an important outcome at work level VI, a world where the corporation is well regarded. This makes it possible to determine investment priorities and to ensure good will and long-term survival and success.

For a work level VI group executive to emerge, one or more of the companies must be a work level V entity. Group executives at this level must ensure connectivity and compliance in three key areas.

Compliance—corporate values and policies and law. Their task is not the what or the why, but the how profits are made.

Capital Allocation—This is a leadership challenge that is not found at any of the other levels since here the GE holds various business accountable for delivering agreed upon profits and strategically allocates corporate capital among the different businesses. To do this, group executives at this work level must have a broad scope and a more objective view than say a level V business CEO who advocates a particular product stream, market, or segment. GEs must determine which products have growth potential and become skilled at sophisticated financial analysis.

Strategic Differentiation—This involves deciding which business has the best strategy and is most closely aligned to corporate strategy and therefore which should be fully funded. The objective is to create the right mix of investments in a number of businesses. This means understanding the pros and cons of growing one business at the expense of another.

The work of Warren Buffet and Charlie Monger piloting Berkshire Hathaway is a modern-day example of stable level VI management. Buffet himself says that his only skills are in the allocation of capital and in choosing those who will run his companies. This downplays his and Monger's other contributions which are about ensuring his companies are run with integrity (compliance) and in terms of deciding which markets he will allocate capital (strategic differentiation).

This is a big step for the newly appointed executive who in the past has valued wealth-creating strategies for an individual business. Now they have to manage a portfolio strategy. Work at this level may be likened to a chief intelligence officer who is constantly reviewing the broad global environment to try and identify and comprehend what is going on—be it economic, social, political, environmental, and technological contexts. She needs to discern what is important for the strategic business units that belong to the group (work level V strategic entities). It requires networking in all areas which are likely to be significant and an understanding of trends beyond the world of the institution. There is a quantum jump from work level V to VI and from III to IV.

It involves stepping outside of a unified system for the first time and dealing with the needs of multiple unified systems. Work at this level is accountable for the delivery of integrated annual and longer term regional and international plans.

It is also accountable for broad scanning so as to be alert and to form intelligence about relevant national and global contexts. *Specific issues arise for action or influencing or observing so as to be able to protect and stimulate or foster conditions for activities in the unified systems that make up a level VI portfolio*. There can be a huge diversity amongst different level V business entities in different global locations, and one needs to be active aware of the activities and practices of suppliers, strategic partners, and alliances, since unfavourable publicity and accusations spread damage around. Thus the executives operating at this level are looking for ways to maintain and enhance relationships. The work level VI executive will help sustain a living context for his or her vice-presidents/divisional MDs and take an active part in the modification and development of corporate strategy. He or she will also ensure that the corporation is moving towards 'clean and green' and is a respected corporate citizen and thus wins growing public opinion in this regards or avoids the negative publicity of being targeted by activists.

A group executive's role is a challenging one. It is often described as a non-job, since after leading a level V business, this role is all about influencing and shaping and taking satisfaction out of others' success.

One level VI chairman described it thus:

'We have the fourth largest turnover on the Stock Exchange. It is important to create a group vision. Almost a behaviours mission. I used to go to the boardrooms of the CEOs of subsidiary companies and their strategy sessions. I used to listen more than participate.

'As Group Chairman I didn't like to put in too much. I liked to provide support, give a bit of direction, but not really interfere. If you try and look for independent result-orientated individuals to run companies, if you recruit people like this, you cannot mould them to yourself.

'You can only hope to infect them with the group values. You hold them responsible for the bottom line and for living up to the values. Of course some of these values cost on the bottom line, but these are the trade-offs. There are always trade-offs down the organisation. It is sometimes five or more years before you see the results, and it is expensive, and it does impact on the bottom line.

'Each of these businesses had their own visions and their own executives that reported to me. I could not force them into using the Corporate vision, but I encouraged them to share it. There was only one thing I insisted upon—the same standards of business ethics and people relationships'.[54]

Decision-Making

Work at this level calls for a wide understanding of global events and trends. It calls for multidimensional thinking and integrating a variety of business needs and issues into a holistic plan. Business units are alerted to the shifts and changes and future implications are *previewed.*

Global competition means that national interests must be contextualised within an increasingly wide and often international sphere of influence. Jobholders normally base their judgement upon taking account of *the known, the expected,* and *the unexpected.* Here one is likely to move between what is anticipated and what is actually happening, much like the general manager at work level IV in devising business plans to achieve a strategic intent.

But now, it is not a single BU or function, it is multiple unified work systems that are involved. All sources and trends may be considered—the expected and unexpected—all provide input into creating understanding of likely sources of strategic opportunities, options, potential instabilities, and vulnerabilities across the group.

Scenario planning for complex companies is found at this work level, and a classic example is the Shell Scenario Planning, *which was a level VII initiative,* and which spread from Shell into other areas such as nation building in South Africa and Ireland.

Time Span

The *Time to Impact of Decision-making* becomes another dimension for consideration at work level VI because of the need to integrate and manage a portfolio of business, and the need for ensuring resilience of these entities into the future.

Consequence of decision-making is also time dependent, and time to impact is defined as *the amount of elapsed time before the outcome of the most complex decision can be confirmed.* This means that the amount of time between completion of the most complex task (the time span) and being able to clearly identifying trends, patterns, and results that confirm or dispute the judgement used in the execution of the task.

The time to impact of decision becomes valid at this level, since it may be between ten and twenty years before some of the decisions can be fully evaluated or even understood. This is often measured by investments in resource replenishment, research and development, and capital infrastructure projects. However, much of the work on this level can have a short-term impact on the viability and vulnerability of the strategic unit, and time spans may be much less.

Creativity and Vulnerabilities

The creativity lies in the understanding and appraisal of the particular situation of each strategic unit and where it fits the strategic vision of the whole. For example, creating strategies for translating the opportunities represented by the siloed markets that exist within the group or international supply-chains linkages and what this represents for potential leverage opportunities.

Thus like any intelligence function, the objective is to inform these entities about possible developments, opportunities and threats, and the financial and other implications thereof. It may be developing a platform across these entities to ensure leverage.

Issues of image and reputation mean representing the organisation in the global arena and being mindful of policies and practices within the unified systems that may cause embarrassment or damage to the greater whole and its purpose.

Changes to whole systems may be initiated at this level, which will involve significant resource configurations.

Organisational Structure

The structure is typically made up of a portfolio of business in different geographical areas. The businesses may be multiple brands, diverse or core. They may differ in complexity and in ownership, but one of which must be a full work level V entity. (Refer Principle 2, Figure 6.)

Leadership

Leadership here is being able to exercise catalysing effects across cultures and groups at a deep level.

This level of leadership is exercised across various operating companies, groups, and divisions. Sustainability and social responsibility issues have pushed the need for this type of leadership high onto the corporate agenda. Increasingly, diverse environments will be part of the play in which national and regional politicians as well institutions and international bodies will become important actors.

At a corporate level, one is able to accomplish difficult, large-scale change repeatedly and well. Leadership is about leading businesses and/or global business streams.

Resources to Be Managed and Performance

Resource management involves overseeing profit and loss in a number of business units and assessing their overall value as reflected in the corporate balance sheet. This includes the assessment of the needs of individual business units for increases or decreases in investment or divestment.

Resources need to be allocated amongst the networks of companies and capital projects, which are not company specific, must be funded. This would involve modifying priorities and requirements of companies and their national contexts to achieve group objectives.

Information gleaned may result in judging investment priorities and deciding when it is appropriate to recommend disinvestment and withdrawal and when to create context and linkages for embedding new business units in new markets.

Performance at this work level is the ability to dominate an entire field, sustaining a position over an extended period of time. This may include regularly winning top competitions, awards, and accolades while remaining an attractive investment opportunity and being a leader in innovation.

Case StudyTesco

Tesco introduced levels of work in the mid-nineties project with a board member as project champion and linked pay bands/recruitment and competencies to all the levels.

They restructured their business into six work levels with their board and CEO occupying level VI. The logo (right) is that used by Tesco for introducing levels of work and below is a fairly bland description of the unique value add of each work level[55]

You will note they have customers at the top of the levels of work hierarchy which is a good reminder of how all work is embedded in the context within which we operate. They describe their work levels as follows:

- *Work level 1:* Front-line jobs working directly with customers. Various in-store tasks such as filling shelves with stock. Requires the ability to work accurately and with enthusiasm and to interact well with others.
- *Work level 2:* Leading a team of employees who deal directly with customers. Requires the ability to manage resources, to set targets, to manage, and to motivate others.
- *Work level 3:* Running an operating unit. Requires management skills including planning, target setting, and reporting.
- *Work level 4*: Supporting operating units and recommending strategic change. Requires good knowledge of the business, the skills to analyse information and to make decisions, and the ability to lead others.

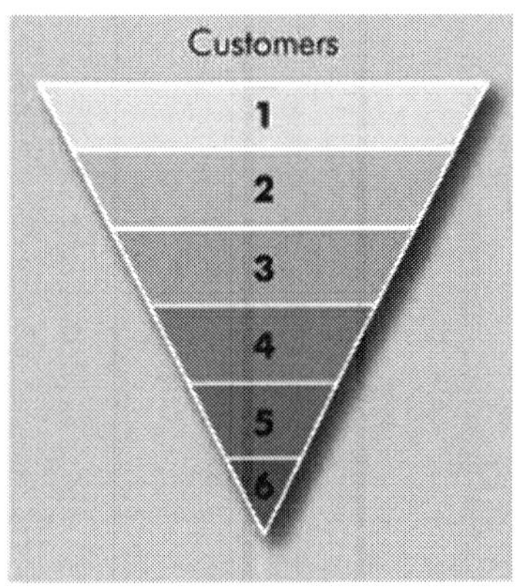

- *Work level 5:* Responsible for the performance of Tesco as a whole. Requires the ability to lead and direct others and to make major decisions.
- *Work level 6:* Creating the purpose, values, and goals for Tesco plc. Responsible for Tesco's performance. Requires a good overview of retailing, and the ability to build a vision for the future and lead the whole organisation.

The CEO Terry Leahy who met and probably exceeded Principle 6 changed the business model from being followers of rivals Sainsbury and Marks & Spencer to becoming a leader. To facilitate his plans, he wanted a transparent, fair system for grading, people development, and a more efficient structure that would serve the customer without distracting people.

It was introduced into ten countries with meticulous planning and full-time project team led by line management. Tesco had also embarked on a policy of international expansion, buts its HR was fragmented and people management systems were not equipped to deal with a growth programme.

Fieldwork was undertaken at Tesco to determine how many levels of decision-making accountability existed and how many were needed. The fieldwork involved face to face interviews from the bottom up in people-intensive area of stores and distribution as well major head office departments, buying, commercial, etc, and the CEO was included.

From this, the required number of decision-making levels was ascertained. They uncovered many, poorly designed and sub-optimal structures, some with too many or too few layers. Pay scales were subsequently shrunk to one band for each work level. Tesco tried out the restructure with a pilot project in a head office department which led into what they called a roll-out plan, supported by HR, and led by line. By 1999, TESCO was voted the UK's most admired company.

Fractal Patterns

Work level VI can be viewed as a fractal pattern of work levels II and IV. Benoit Mandelbrot won a Nobel Prize for his discovery of a new geometry—fractals. Nature, it was found, has a way of using resources sparingly—to do more with less. Fractals are reoccurring, iterative pattern of complexity in which a simple pattern or design is used over and over again with increasing complexity. This is nature acting both frugally and with abundance.

Levels of work have fractal qualities or repetitions of patterns, which, when carefully introduced, brings a simplicity into design that is resilient to changing circumstances. It provides type of genetic code into the architecture, design, or structure helping to ensure resilience and viability.

Consider that fractals exist in this complexity-based approach to work.

Work level II, work level IV, and work level VI are fractals of one another, reiterated at higher levels of complexity. The common thread is that they all involve *translation to identify what needs to happen*. At work level II, the Service work theme, a Front-Line Manager or specialist is responsible for resolving or identifying a particular situation within the requirements of the local context. This is focus on a specific area or unit of work. It may involve a great deal of detail and interactions between the parts. It is likely to have a defined outcome, be it in achieving customer satisfaction, settling a shop floor disagreement, improving a process, winning a technical court case, or successfully completing a surgical procedure.

At work level IV, an executive is responsible for spanning a broad spectrum of level III Practices that may exist across a number of processes or delivery systems. Here the focus must be across a broad spectrum of specifics. In terms of the operation of the business unit or area of responsibility, what should be happening, what is not happening, and what needs to be happening? She or he may focus in on specific aspects that require attention in the context of the overall situation as pertains to the strategic or business plans for the business unit. Thus the particular at work level II has now become specifics of a number of systems or processes and set in a broader more complex context. The specific has become broader and more complex.

For work in IV, the information which needs to be gathered spans the organisation and into the external context and informs the decision in the face of the unknown whereas in work level II information is gathered about the particular situation and is often used to justify course of action.

In work theme of Corporate Citizenship, the corporate executive is responsible for obtaining intelligence from a broad range of sources on political, economic, and social fronts in order to alert particular business units to possible opportunities, dangers, and developments. The fractal component has moved from the complexity of localised work specifics to specifics within a unified system often contextualised within a broad operating context—to become 'specifics' that are often emergent and which span a broad range of environments, audiences, and diversity. This is why scenario planning is such an effective strategic tool at this work level.

The fractal nature of work takes a simple concept, in this example that of dealing with a specific and resolving it, to an increasingly broader perspective, but that the *essential concept underlying the pattern remains the same*. Thus the idea of thinking globally and acting locally is given greater relevance here. The specifics are issues which impact on one or more unified work systems, in one or multiple geographic sites, and may impact on an entire value chain. For example, environmentally unfriendly logging practices that activists have targeted may impact an entire value chain from forest to retail shops.

A Note on the History of the Work Level VI

This is the first work level which lies in the heart of the Values Domain and is about sensing needs of human society and increasingly not only from a commercial base with its mantra of 'limitless growth'.

It is a level of work that should take responsibility for the broader agenda that includes shaping human culture and values and that does not mean every table has a tin of Coke and a McDonald hamburger or every person has an iPad. It is increasingly about the management of human culture through fostering tolerance and diversity and creating *non zero sum games* where benefits are handed out and vulnerabilities shared through consensus and risk taking.

It is about seeing the continuance of human existence through awareness of environmental degradation and that the global business model has to change. Profit can no longer be king. The canvas has grown substantially broader, and the stage is increasingly being jostled by new players other than the chairpersons and CEOs of commercial global players or the leaders of governments unable to change or adapt. The world is awash in new information and knowledge and for group executives to ignore this signs, may prove the kiss of death to their sustainability.

Many companies[56] have come under the spotlight for not being corporate citizens or playing in murky waters. British Aerospace avoided allegations of licensing weapon plants to repressive regimes. Cargill, a huge grain trader, accused of promoting genetically modified seeds and damaging the Bolivian coast also escaped being brought to justice because of the secretive nature of its structure. Apple, with its factories in China, is another recent example, although product demand has overruled ethical considerations for many.

A major component of work at this level is looking at and monitoring alternative meanings that might arise for an enterprise in a range of scenarios. These scenarios represent preferred, acceptable, and, importantly, non-preferred futures.

Case Study Continue
Building a Corporation

The Growth of Virgin Through the Levels of Work Lens

Richard Branson's cognitive power (CP) saw him transition to work level VI in his late thirties and early forties. Transitions represent a gradual shift in thinking. Increased complexity of the business would again follow this cognitive growth. As if to confirm that transition in 1992, at forty-two, Branson sold his most profitable and successful part of his empire, Virgin Music, for close to $1 billion. This sale would mark a dramatic shift in focus from its core business of entertainment towards airlines and travel. The sale also provided capital to support new business ventures.

The clarity of purpose for Branson himself came in his previous cycle, evolving during the eight to ten years in work level V where he first became involved in travel. His involvement and passion about travel saw him participate in speedboat races and air-balloon competitions, and winning major awards. This publicity did much to build and reinforce his brand, confirming and sealing his passion in travel.

This new cycle of capability growth brought with it a need to play on a global canvas. For Branson, this transition honed his ability to see gaps and create new businesses (and indeed a whole new industry). Here, one accumulates information and synthesise it in a way that allows one to sit back (and oxymoron with the person in question) to consider nascent trends and not so obvious links and, in some cases, to surface them and turn them into ventures. James Lovelock formulated his Gaia hypothesis in this work level (after years of testing and information collecting) and took it to the world. It is also the work level where Muhammad Yunus rolled out his microfinance concepts to the world in his fight against poverty. A new industry was born, and microfinance was soon replicated in seventy different countries. This foresight, in most cases, is subconscious but has a conscious reaction in identifying possibilities and opportunities in countries within industries or globally.

Branson commented in his book Business Stripped Bare *when in 1999, he registered Virgin Galactic that he had for years '. . . been keeping tabs on anything and everything to do with the vexed business of getting off the ground and into space. I wanted to be the first in this sector . . . this is the unseen part of business, the part that nobody ever discusses because to be fair, there not a lot to discuss. The secret to success in any new sector is watchfulness, usually over a period of many years . . . Virgin's sudden emergence as a leader in cutting edge industries was decades in the making. You need a huge amount of sheer curiosity to make it in a new sector.'*[57]

The year 1995 saw an acceleration of business development opportunities. There was a plethora of new ventures in diverse markets globally, which could only be identified and leveraged from work level VI. Virgin responded to three types of opportunities—privatisation and deregulation—which saw Virgin Blue enter Australia, Virgin Express in Europe, an unsuccessful bid for the British National Lottery, and Virgin Atlantic. The underlying rational was looking for opportunities created by moribund industries and monopolies that would respond to a competitive value proposition for consumers.

On the UK home front 1995 also saw Virgin Direct being launched offering telephone-based financial services to clients. Virgin Car and Virgin Bike followed which offered direct sales of cars and motorbikes at discounted prices. Virgin Direct was a JV with the Australian AMP and later changed its name to Virgin Money.

The third area that Virgin was involved in was what was referred to as TMT (technology, media, and telecommunications), which caused great excitement in Virgin. The Internet offered new ways to connect to the customer, and in 1997, Virgin Net was launched, and the next year Virgin Mobile with half a million customers within first year and four million by 2004. This huge response form the market encouraged Richard, who expanded into the US, Australia, and SE Asia. The Internet allowed Virgin to communicate directly with customers and text messaging allowed Virgin Atlantic to sell discount seats to Virgin Mobile customers.

In 1996, Virgin Rail was set up to bid for operating franchises in the British Rail system, and by 1997, it was operating two rail companies although it was not to be a happy story for some time to come.

The Virgin Entertainment Group comprised all Virgin retailing businesses together with Virgin cinema chains. Profitability of this group was reported as miserable, and it was struggling by 2004.

This diverse business activity allowed Branson to sell off equity stakes in some of his more established ventures including 49 per cent of Virgin Atlantic to Singapore Airlines for over £600 million.

The rapid diversification of the nineties and the spread of Virgin to Australia, Europe, and elsewhere all called for cash demands. These demands plus those of the railways, retailing, and financial services made it necessary to look for external equity funding. This resulted in Branson attracting investment using the tools of the trade such as venture capital, JV partners, and IPOs.

His public image and current effective level of work allowed him to attract outside investors. Branson's high profile, network of connections, and celebrity status allowed him promote new ventures and to acquire equity quite disproportionate to the size of Virgin's financial investment which was normally fairly small.

By this stage Virgin was a conglomerate of relatively small, nimble independent organisations being led from work levels III to V. Overall Branson led a corporate core at Work Level VI that that played an active role in certain key businesses while continually boundary scanning for new opportunities. Values, brand and personal leadership charisma (the Temperament factor) acted as the glue that bound this enterprise together.

(Continued in Work Level VII)

Case Study Continued
Building a Social Entrepreneurial Business

The Growth of the Grameen Bank Through the Levels of Work Framework

In a different part of the world, Muhammed Yunus completed his Ph.D. in economics in the US and returned to the newly independent Bangladesh. He resigned a government role and took up an academic post as an economics professor. With the Bangladesh famine, he questioned how the global economic system failed humanity and devised an alternative banking system to help the poor. This new approach he grew steadily through a number of joint ventures.

His cognitive growth into this new cycle ushered in the capability for work level VI challenges. His activities in this work level is best summarised as follows:

Consolidation and institutional growth.

Diversification and replication of Grameen activities globally and increasing recognition of his vision. Here the organisational growth model was not acquisitions but networked proliferation where numerous other independent entities would try out and then adopt the methodologies of Grameen.

Work level VI saw him bedding down the work he had done while at the same time expanding the model globally wherever he could find a foothold and welcome. He wanted to spread the message, and this is an example of an individual in work level VI, shaping an industry to the new rules of a new game with a new language.

Yunus visited Chicago in 1985 to talk to activist groups, and it proved to be a novel experience. The groups felt that an experiment in Bangladesh had no relevance to the US with its sophisticated markets and institutional structures. However, two people believed in the idea, and in 1985, started a Grameen-type operation in Chicago. Yunus challenged institutions such as the World Bank, the role of international donor aid and consultants and how they failed to really change the lot of the poor. His ideas were also growing internationally with organisations replicating the Grameen formulae with slow but steady success. In 1986, operations were set up in Malaysia and Norway. Yunus again visited the US and met with Governor Clinton and Hilary who both became supporters.

In 1990, as he transitioned again, he made a landmark speech entitled 'Anything Wrong?' on the problems of banking worldwide. The concepts and ideas of the Grameen Bank continued to grow through replication in Canada and in, 1991, South America. His work in the US also continued, and in 1991, he set a target of raising $100 over five years, followed by a target of reaching the poorest 100 million by 2006.

(Continued in Work Level VII)

Work Level VII

Also Known as Corporate Prescience

Unique Purpose of the Work

This Level of Work complexity has two primary functions.

Firstly, the creation of the new. In its simplest term, this work level is about anticipating and establishing new unified business systems that serve society's future needs. This is accomplished through alliances, mergers, acquisitions, or building them. The BHP Billiton merger could be seen as a level VII decision as it brought about a new multinational economic and social entity.

Secondly, the work is about 'maintaining' the established unified groupings of 'whole' systems. This maintaining determines how value can be established and enhanced across all of the activities. Jobholders and the boards need to define what the lasting needs of the company are and assist the chairman in establishing a long-term core strategy. They also need to ensure performance is in line with the strategy for their watch. It is important that elements of the strategy are transferable and sustainable over the long haul.

Work level VII is accountable for decisions taken to develop or transform work level V business units as well as divest of others for strategic reasons.

Thus a level VII executive is responsible for ensuring amalgamated profit and losses, balance sheets, image and reputation, and growth of the brand name globally for the parent organisation and its local and strategic business units. They proactively position and create institutions and businesses across the globe to enhance the region and group.

Decision-Making

The board and CEO must identify and set priorities to ensure the maximum use is made of finite resources in achieving key opportunities and objectives. This decision-making process is geared to meet key business drivers which are sustained profit and wealth creation for the long term, while contextually considering issues of social and ethical responsibility, environmental sustainability, and global development opportunity.

Judgement making is based on interpreting the shifting probabilities not of the given but of the emergent or hidden contexts of nations, alliances, local groupings, polities, economic, and environmental trends that remain as yet undefined. Factors such as these represent the source material, which the person will use to shape desired futures.

As at all levels, uncertainty is the raw material for making judgement, but here, uncertainty is not perceived as an unknown. It is viewed as intrinsically unknowable and therefore malleable.

People comfortable operating in this level of capability generate images and designs for new forms of social and economic institutions that will contribute in as yet undefined forms.

Conceptual pathways composed of the sequential use of theoretical models is deployed to understand and construct potential open systems or4th Order Universals, such as post-capitalism, colonialism, democracy, global warming, limits to growth, sustainability, civil society, philosophical, judicial, ethical and value systems.[2]

Time Span

Twenty years plus as agreed by board and group CEO is what is put forward by Jaques. However, from a more practical point of view, the

---

2 Ibid.

impact of decision-making may be above ten years but not exceeding fifty years.

Organisational Structure

This level of decision-making brings into being new unified work systems and forms of social, economic, and political institutions. Chairs, boards, and CEO are often found at this level. Jaques speaks about stratum VI and VII as belonging to the corporate collegiate in that the issues being dealt impact many players from diverse interest groups. Part of the core of work level at this level is judging the needs of current and nascent societies and regional groupings and deciding on what types of strategic entities to provide in the future to satisfy them.

Work is focussed on sustainable wealth creation in its broadest sense. Level VII work has been subject to the most dramatic pressures in the last thirty years as real-time technology, higher education levels, environmental pressures, and the growth of a global 'meshed' brain continue to raise levels of governance, involvement, and consequences of actions.

Leadership

Leadership here is being able to articulate ideas of millions, facilitate, and catalyse identity on a massive scale.'

It is about being able to translate currents of emotions, needs, and patterns, both felt and nascent into forces of paradigm change. The need to satisfy markets and shareholders has seen real leadership at this level being dumbed down to meet market demands.

Capability for this level of leadership and beyond makes up a small talent pool. It is found among thought leaders and not for profits, international bodies, advisors, and activists, although many do not belong to 'accountable work systems'. Here one is able to catalyse historic changes by leading millions of people to grasp problems or opportunities, be it through the dissemination of new knowledge, new ideas, and embodying it with its own language. Two examples are Aung San Suu Kyi and Nelson Mandela.

Unfortunately, this level of leadership has not always been used for good over the history of humanity and its reduction to one mostly geared around economic advantage has seen its broader value increasingly undermined. The abuse of the Value Domain for unfair advantage has seen mass protest arise such as the 2011 Occupy Wall Street movement.

The capability associated with those comfortable to work at this level is prescience and is about revealing the future to others. Often this is the culmination of a process of discovery that starts in work level V, growing and developing until it emerges on the global stage as a new force with a new language. It represents the ability to re-interpret the present and to create a new future—one complete with a new language and values which will encompass many areas of human activity and knowledge.

So it has been with the language of James Lovelock and Gaia[58] *and all of its implications. The implications of Gaia are profound, not only from shaping a new unifying theory of multidisciplinary science but also in the domain of shaping human culture and values at a global level. The concept of Gaia like that of microcredit may be developed and existing cultures shaped. Actors on this stage are aware that they are at the root of important development and may know each other, debating issues with passion. These new values systems are supported by epistemological and a systems based approach.*

Case Study Continued
Building a Corporation

The Growth of Virgin Through the Levels of Work Lens

Is it a coincidence that as Branson transitioned in work level VII, he set up Virgin Galactic, a private company? He was the first to go boldly into a whole new industry of space tourism. As he mentioned earlier, he has kept an eye on all things that fly and go into space. The background to this is that with the demise of the Soviet Union, Margaret Thatcher had remarked to Gorbachov that Branson was an interesting person to meet and who might be able to help with the establishment of a free market economy. Branson on a trip to Russia was invited to visit Star City, home of the Soviet and now Russian Federation space industry. Here, he was offered the opportunity to be the first civilian to go into space but with *a price tag of $30 million. He turned it down. The cost horrified him, although some eight individual's to date have visited the International Space Station and have paid this price tag. This got Branson thinking, and he commented, 'Half a dozen people in space at a total cost of nearly $200 million—that isn't very good, is it?'*

Branson considered space tourism a real possibility and it was a foundation that could lead to many other possibilities ' . . . the business to include environmental work in space, satellite payload launching and astronaut training . . . I wanted to see if the taking people into space could become a working business proposition and also create a new technological platform for science, satellites and other human activities in space. There is no doubt though that tourists need to be the first stepping stone on our journey' (see endnote lvii). *Here is a long-term view about creating the conditions for a fledgling industry to expand rapidly. Until very recently, space has been in the national domain of governments. This is clearly an area where Branson saw long-term advantages to entering a 'new market' that would allow him to not only create a strong lead but spearhead a major wave of human development.*

This type of industry creation is only amenable to entry at work level V because of the high costs and barriers to entry. It is not like Bill Gates or Muhammad Yunus who grew new industries from scratch, initially at little or low cost, before exploding onto the global scene when they transitioned into work level V. This industry is a playing field that you can only enter through one of two portals; either your working journey over the decades has taken you there (you have the wealth to play which was made somewhere else) or you create an invention that so revolutionises the industry that your access pass is a lifelong membership. It may be argued that Branson's initial entry into this industry could be traced back to work level V. Since it was shortly after he transitioned into this work level he found his wings and soared with Virgin Atlantic and in his balloons! In reality though, he bought his way with a calculated risk.

In 1999, he registered Virgin Galactic. 'The last week of September 2004 is one I will always cherish. We launched our 125 mph Pendolino tilting service in the UK. We gained plaudits from the President of Nigeria for the launch of Virgin Nigeria. And I was on the platform at the Royal

Organisational Design Aeronautical Society in London with Burt to announce the launch of Virgin Galactic.'[57]

People who are comfortable with this level of capability are able to see what is or might be needed on a global scale as their 'focus' encapsulates the diverse contexts within which their business are operating. While many can easily imagine space travel, it takes this level of capability to see what therefore needs to happen next and to then make it happen. It is no coincidence that these two work levels belong to what has been so aptly named the 'Values Domain'.[59]

Branson after meeting Mandela had been so captivated by his wisdom, inspirational leadership, and natural entrepreneurial ability that he formed a deep relationship with the man and the country. He bought an ailing health and fitness group, and Virgin Active was born amongst a host of other initiatives.

An opportunity arose for Branson to broker a meeting of President Mandela and the Dalai Lama in that magical year of 2004. The meeting of these two great minds resulted in the development of an idea to bring together a group of wise global Elders to use their wisdom and capability to address pressing global issues. The Elders could do things the UN could not. Branson said, 'As the United Nations represents the nations of the world, the Elders would represent the hopes, aspirations, fears and dreams of the people.'

Hoebeke contends that those with the capability to transition beyond work level VII enter a space where work as we know it does not exist but that the nature of its activities becomes spiritual, the home of Jaques's Extraordinary and Legendary Mortals. One may well argue that the Elders are such a collegial grouping in theory at least. The author's analysis of the working journeys of Nelson Mandela, Muhammad Yunus, and Jimmy Carter[60] *indicates that all possess the cognitive power to move into this spiritual domain, as does Richard Branson.*

It was in the same year that Branson realised the need to pull all the social responsibility work that the Virgin Group (200 affiliated companies, employing some 50,000 people in 29 countries) was doing under one umbrella. He created Virgin Unite as his non-profit foundation. It objectives were to tackle social and environmental problems through an entrepreneurial approach by creating a new way for business and the social sector to work together.

Virgin Unite, with Branson's active support then, went out to create the funds, set up infrastructure and think tanks with leaders such as ex-President Carter, Archbishop Despond Tutu, and many others to bring the Elders[61] *into creation. Nelson Mandela was the founding elder. Branson hopes the body will still exist in a hundred years' time and says, 'The Elders are, in essence, a group of immensely influential world figures acting like entrepreneurs who use their moral courage, wisdom and independent leadership to tackle huge intractable problems. The beauty of the Elders is that they are at a time in their careers where they have no other agenda but that of humanity.* [61]

At this stage of his working journey, Branson is working across a wide portfolio of diverse interests, focussing on specific areas but acting to empower others and creating the conditions for businesses of the Virgin brand and others to be successful globally. A scan of his portfolio makes interesting reading, and the most marvellous outline of this is in the inside jacket covers of his book Business Stripped Bare *is simply Branson's 'to-do' list. This gives a full range of activities across multiple business units in multiple countries.*

In 2004 the Virgin Group of companies comprised several holding companies and over 200 operating companies, many of which were based within Britain, the equity was owned by Branson, both individually and through a series of trusts is held by Virgin Investment Group. How this loose confederation is held together is an example of a complex adaptive system that holds true to some of the Requisite Laws. The glue that holds it together is the Virgin Trademark. His unique value add as one might expect is primarily in publicity, public and government relations and critically, the appointment of senior executives and willingness to act if they are not achieving.

Despite the diversity, Virgin companies possess an entrepreneurial culture and follow strategies based upon novel approaches for creating value for the consumers. As group CEO, it is Richards's role and UVA to be the exemplar of these values and culture. Virgin Group is almost a pure branding operation. It licenses the Virgin brand name to many of the businesses in the Virgin family, choosing to remain at something of a distance to the actual operating companies. In many instances (such as Virgin Mobile in Australia, which is owned by Singtel Optus), the arrangement is little more than a brand licence agreement.[62]

Work level VII is a truly global work level, and it is the work level where the global CEO will examine opportunities to embed businesses in different countries, through buy, build, or JVs. It is where they create conditions for all the businesses to flourish through creating goodwill and building reputation and image. It is also where significant investments can be made for creating the market conditions for new industries to be successful.

A word of warning . . . Principle 4 states that one role must not report to another in the same work level. A derivative of this principle is that of the 'missing' work level shown in Figure 11 (example C). Consider how difficult it will be working with a CEO in work level VII (or above), who will not want to be involved in the affairs of work level V entities to the degree required. He may also not want to be actively engaged in the management of his team at work level VI as a Manager or MoR any longer.

This has serious implications for sustainability as key business issues will not be addressed such as performance, tasking, and business leadership. It also makes the assumption that the executive team is capable to operate in work level VI (Principle 6 states people who are capable to add value must be deployed to the appropriate level of work complexity) and many organisations have not managed this effectively. For example, if his executive team is comfortable with work level V, then there may theoretically be two missing work levels.

For those with the capability to grow through work level VII, the issue is how to manage such unusual CEOs. Bill Gates got out, leaving Microsoft in the hands of a CEO arguably at the right work level. Yunus plays on a different stage, leaving the operations of Grameen Bank at the appropriate level, while he furthers the message on the global stage.

One can only hope Branson has done likewise.

(End of case study)

Case Study Continued
Building a Social Entrepreneurial Business

The Growth of the Grameen Bank Through the Levels of Work Lens

The story of the Grameen Bank is another example which we first encountered in the discussion of level V work. Yunus found that his alternative banking system worked, and in the course of its growth created a new banking institution with the new language of microcredit. But the institutional objective was not profit; it was the eradication of poverty. In its process of growth, the Grameen Bank had become a model for other similar institutions and had evolved into a networked group of entities at work level VII.

In 1990, Yunus made a landmark speech entitled 'Anything Wrong?' on the problems of banking worldwide, taking specific aim at a world awash with money while poverty was rampant. By 1991, the concepts and ideas of the Grameen Bank had grown through replication into Canada and in 1991 South America. His work in the US also continued, and in 1991, he set a target of raising $100 over five years, followed by a target of reaching the poorest 100 million by 2006.

By 1996, the Grameen Bank had issues a total of $151 million dollars' worth of housing loans, and the first microcredit summit was held. It was an historical event that was attended by many international public figures and leaders.

In 1998, the Grameen Bank had 12,000 employees, 2.3 million customers, and 1112 branches. Replication of the Grameen model was across more than 59 countries. By comparison, in January 2007, it has 6.95 million borrowers, 97 per cent of whom are women, and 2,343 branches. GB provides services in 75,359 villages, covering more than 90 per cent of the total villages in Bangladesh.

Finally, after a long history of disagreements, a World Bank study concluded Grameen was a sound, viable, and worthwhile institution.

In 2006, he shared the Nobel Peace Prize with the Grameen Bank.

(End of case study)

A New Work Level in a New Domain?

Figure 17: Our species is covering the globe.
Earth at night (Images courtesy of: DMSP and NASA.)[63]

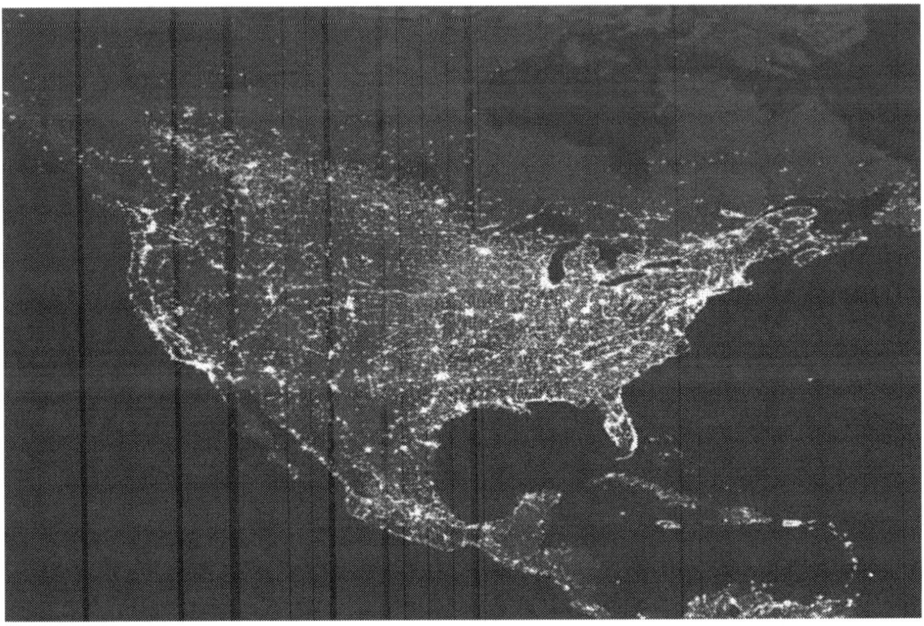

Work Level VIII

Also Known as Corporate Sustainability

Societal growth has reached a point where the way we have lived and worked is increasingly unable to reconfigure to meet a raft of deeply complex challenges. Arguably, it is the role of the leader to create the future and to ensure life and order continue in the face of the unknowable. If so, some might think their performance has let us down. The contentious work level VIII, as yet ill-defined seeks to operate in the 50-100 year-time frames, where what has been provides little or no guide to the century ahead.

Companies battle to think in the long term. They face a continuous and grinding need for growth and to continuously produce profits. Some battle for survival, while others have grown fat from their past successes and from tax payer bailouts when they should have failed. It is not surprising that the average time span of decision-making of significant enterprises is five to seven years for almost all but the largest of companies. Many level V organisations operate with three year survival tactics.

Some colleagues argue that work level VIII is the domain of the supersized work level VII companies, distinguished by mammoth size, revenue, reach, and diversity of purpose. For example, measuring on this scale, the resource giant ExxonMobil may belong here as well as the energy company Shell, who has an illustrious history in envisaging alternative futures. Walmart the world's eighteenth largest public corporation with over two million employees may also join the list.[64]

Jaques's description of work level VII as 'Direct Multiple Unified Systems in the Global Environment' makes pragmatic sense and still refers to shareholders returns as the significant measure of success. The UVA of work level VIIII has not been clearly defined in such terms. Caution needs to be exercised in simple extrapolations.

Jaques was also clear that work in the formal sense is where X holds Y accountable for delivering specific outputs within a specific time and that type of work is found in organisations called Accountable Hierarchies.

Accountable Hierarchies are created by associations, normally comprised of shareholders (be it a company, a nation, a trade union). But societal complexity in the twenty-first century is demanding more than delivering profits to its shareholders while avoiding accountability for the real cost of doing business.

Now we all face a world where cold winds of uncertainty are gathering strength.

The existence of future generations living in the manner many of us have grown accustomed to is under threat. Part of the planet may become uninhabitable due to our need for continuous growth and the cost of this to the environment. Leadership, at this point in time, seem incapable of producing a comprehensive approach to deal with the complexity that we face. All appears to be in flux, yet there is a sense of momentous change in the offing.

Never before has our impact been planetary and never before has there been so many striving for a first-world lifestyle. The GFC, poverty, climate change, biodiversity extinction, peak oil, and a rising population of seven billion seem to work against the best efforts of global leadership. The context of nation states (a nineteenth-century institution) and the never-ending need to follow policies of job creation, competitive growth, and economic advantage erodes the high-level leadership required. The GFC and its aftermath brought home how human society cannot continue to function effectively without growth fuelling its consumer based economy. The mantra is for more growth, more development.

It is abundantly clear that a new form of global leadership and vision is required and that economic growth as the primary measurable cannot be sustained. Jared Diamond in his book *Collapse*[65] traced the demise of ancient societies due to factors which were ignored, misunderstood, or unrealised. Today's society cannot plead ignorance.

We know.

Paul Gilding, in his book *The Great Disruption*[66] believes humanity will act but only at the last moment and only when direct action is required. He envisages a war situation where a global mobilisation is required.

Unlikely. Some systems are broken and parts like Greece may be "lost". More realistically, we will be like the frog not noticing the increased temperature. As Graham Harris, a colleague and eminent scientist commented, 'Apocalypse Not'—but rather a gradual loss of our world and diminished quality of life, and wars, of course. We are in living in the middle of change, a experiment if you wish and work level VIII is still emergent.

What we might assume is that the context for future work at this level goes far beyond the current model of early twenty-first century capitalism. Much of current 'corporate sustainability' is misleading and essentially a window dressing. Its interventions rarely go beyond work level III, and corporate sustainability at the higher work levels would appear by and large to be focussed on ensuring business as usual into the future. However, that is not to say the need for change is not driving technological innovation. It is, but that is unlikely to make the impact required.

It is the context within which business operates that is going to shape Work Level VIII and possibly give rise to a whole new domain of work. The context within which business takes place is being shaped by real and predicted climatic and economic events, the looming prospect of peak oil and the active and ongoing contributions of community activists, popular movements, international bodies and advisors, as they do battle with established institutions, governance and regulatory environments. A new set of values (memes) is already here, and change is steadily and constantly being introduced and with it, a growing awareness of the fragility of our position in the environment.

These new values in turn are seeing the patchy emergence of a different set of dynamics for doing 'business'. It is therefore highly likely that work level VIII will be very different to our traditional work systems and less likely to merely be work level VII supersized.

So what might the UVA of Work Level VIII look like?

The primary objective of work level VIII may be that of 'rewiring' and downsizing the economic engines and institutions of the Industrial Age. A preliminary definition may be 'Coordinate numerous emerging/ established global systems in order to build long-term resilience" This may be accomplished by a new grouping of institutions tasked with transforming the fabric of society into a low carbon and sustainable existence. In essence work level VIII will set about rewiring existing unified systems and creating a new order, with performance measured across multiple capitals.

Such configuration may be concerned with coordinating and integrating functions locally and globally, a fractal of work level IV and VI—but now working to ensure compliance and context for a vast network of smaller, localised work systems, utilising a raft of different financial and capital forms. Some aspects of work at this level may be collaborative development in order to pool resources to fund major capital investements in new infrastructure, technology, education, health and rehabilitation of ecosystems.

It is also possible that work level VIII will emerge for a specific purpose and will collapse when its work is done. As a more mature and assertive society emerges, armed with new group based planetary memes (and there is no gaurantee of successful emergence), work levels VI and VII may implode as the growth mantra loses its preeminence.

It is almost guaranteed that different capitals will become more, if not equally, valued and smaller may well become beautiful as E. E. Schumacher famously said, 'Maybe we are just starting to grow up!'

SECTION III

New Case Studies

Case Study 1

Ericsson India. A Personal Reflection on the Seven Principles of Design

This case study examines how a new executive applied the sequence of events and all the Seven Principles in the restructuring of a business unit.

To me, RO had been an intriguing science and subject of study. Its concepts have always resonated deeply with me and helped to explain what I observed at work.

In 2007, I was appointed Vice-President, Multimedia and Systems Integration, at Ericsson India, and we packed the family bags for Delhi. While the surrounding environment is quite demanding (ranging from poverty to the possibility of food poisoning) for a family with a small baby, the Indian people are just amazingly warm and generous.

The work environment is hectic, pulsating, and intense, and you never know what to expect. I arrived when around 10 million new mobile phone subscribers were added to the networks every month. However, having worked with the headquarter strategies and other markets, I knew that this underlying momentum was not enough to fuel the growth I was assigned to drive.

My purpose was to help the operators of mobile, fixed, and TV networks evolve from basic voice telephony to rich multimedia and applications with the needed support systems. One month after arriving at the new job, I engaged a consulting company's help to ensure that we quickly could get on track. The approach was to

- define exactly what the president wanted to get done—what task? *(Principle 1 and 3: the business intent and time span of decisions.)*
- match the most complex tasks with capability of individuals. *(Principle 6: people must be able to handle the complexity of work.)*
- work together with HR, and define and execute a plan to get the right people matching the delegated tasks with the capability of individuals. (Sequence of events and *Principle 5: empowering roles—authority—capability.*)

The Task

It was important to get a clear picture of what was to be the longest task, that is, what was expected of me and the teams in my organisation. A key contributing factor to defining the longest task was to get the expectations from key stakeholders (customers, my manager—the President of Ericsson India, sales VPs, etc), and once it was defined, a time span was worked out and agreed for the task.

While the task itself was not that difficult to define, it is quite important to stress the value of the process and getting everybody involved. For example, the task really meant to focus a lot on the user experience of our customer's customers, the consumers themselves, and not just rely on the providers/operators. With the effects of Google and Apple's iPhone on our industry during that time (where telecom operators lost power in the value chain), such strategic choice made a large impact.

Another key element of the task was that we did not know when the mobile Internet market would take off and hence had to build our execution having that timing uncertainty in mind. The task was estimated to take seven to eight years (mid-level 5) to complete, but to adjust to the common planning horizon in the unit, we kept talking about five years and beyond.

We defined the task as

Within five years (by 2012), develop Multimedia, SI, and its business models in India, and lead users to attractive multimedia experiences, and become the market leader in solutions and systems integration and support for hosting/managed services thus enabling services for multimedia providers when the market takes off.

Organisation and Capability

To understand how to achieve the task I also required understanding of how the organisational structure had been working and a complete picture of the talent pool.

During the first two weeks, we rated the capability of the top two levels in the unit partly via assessments from the manager and then confirmed by me as MoR and partly via capability interviews (for the high potentials and key contributors).

In the capability interviews, the respondent is asked to reason around a large and fairly general topic, like globalisation, for one hour. The recorded conversation is then analysed to identify the underlying structure of mental processing and then compared with the capability level, for example, parallel processing for work level IV.

Structure and Tasks for the Team

Once we had the task and were clear on what we needed to accomplish, we defined the delegations to the eadership team. For me to be able to achieve my task (at level V), I needed to delegate tasks and roles within level IV with a two to five years perspective. This entailed lifting the work level as it was one full level higher than the previous management team. This led to the conclusion that I needed to both raise the expectations (longer time perspective, higher complexity) as well as add some new people.

The tasks were defined through deep interviews and separate sessions. In addition, we ran a joint workshop for the whole leadership team where each one compared the delegated tasks they had received from me and what they had delegated in turn. This helped in the internalisation part of delegation, a task is nothing if it is not understood and agreed upon.

Once finalised, everyone in the organisation could see how their tasks related to their managers as well as everyone else's. That process was very effective in securing Principle 5 which is about empowering role relationships thorough clear authority and accountability and getting team members to work effectively together.

People

As the level of complexity in the management team was raised, I needed to make some adjustments in the structure of the team, developing and retaining those individuals who could cope with the higher work levels and giving stretch assignment to those that had a higher level of capability. But the capability side was not enough if we were to build great user experiences in a market where telecom meets industries like media and Internet. We could not rely solely on the strong telecom experience in the team. We needed other competencies as well. Hence we started to look externally for people with new and complimentary skill sets and used our new, well-defined task descriptions in the job ads. This helped attract the right people.

Our advertising process was extremely effective, setting an interesting context for applicants, by articulating the tasks with purpose, in an exciting, clear, and dynamic manner. As a result, we managed to attract a completely new range of senior candidates.

What we were looking for were the following:

- Capability level needed to be higher.
  - More complex tasks and longer time span.
  - More maturity to build subunits (MKU and MRU) and effective structures to execute (*Principle 3*).
  - Executive level customer interaction.
- Competence lift needed in new areas (*Principle 6*).
  - Content, media, IT, and integration (not only telecom).
  - Leadership skills and experience.
  - Diversity (gender, industry, market).

- Commitment to end-to-end responsibility.
    - Regardless of organisation. A holistic mindset and a willingness to drive the transformation of our business with the rest of the organisation (a yes-we-can approach).

Aftermath and Effects

While some changes were done directly, some required more time in order not to jeopardise the current business and customers while finding and grooming the new leaders. Remember, one of the primary purposes of work level IV is to maintain current operations while transitioning to the desired future. The result was a leadership team of 11 strong individuals with the right capability and the required competences to help us achieve our objective.

The clarity in the longest tasks was beneficial for my whole organisation. Even people who were deselected for roles, the management team gave positive feedback, and they were motivated to continue to contribute in their new assigned role.

It was nice to see that when I recruited a former CTO from a TV broadcaster, suddenly new candidates started to apply for jobs, and customers asked for meetings. One customer meeting was interrupted as one of the customer participants that knew this new head of TV solutions went out the room and shouted to some colleagues to join, saying, 'Guys, look who is here with Ericsson. Please join'.

Similarly, the new head of Project Management managed to recruit 20 top IT project managers from our top competitors in one year with profiles that we had not seen before even when using the best headhunters.

The team grew from 50 to 200, and we made a fabulous journey that holds a special place in all our hearts, not just for the business achievements but for being in that magical flow that is created where excellent people form one unified team knitted together with strong values. Even several years later, I see photos from family events and team building that people post and share to relive the feeling.

While both financial—and employee-empowerment figures improved substantially, I would like to mention some other effects:

- The new leadership team being perceived as much stronger and more focused.
- Customers asking to meet us where they did not do so before.
- Great cost savings due to better business and domain expertise.
- Ericsson India now asked also to create global functions for Ericsson in multimedia and systems integration.
- A culture where great people hire great people.

So was this team two years later organised perfectly according to the RO science? No. I made small exceptions due to other reasons; for example, using individual to do work above their designated roles where they had very strong skills or great customer relationships, especially in areas where that was the most important thing during that period of time. I believe that the manager needs to make conscious compromises based on a holistic view on what is best for the company in short and long terms.

This leads to some key observations and learning:

- People are OK with taking a smaller role if it is clear why.
- People are OK with not being selected but tell them right away.
- Honest and clear feedback from the manager—a basic human right and one that lies at the heart of RO—building a strong, trusting two-way relationship for great business outcomes.
- Employees, managers, and customers—all can intuitively feel the capability of your people and will judge you accordingly.
- Be opportunistic about great people. Never completely close the door for recruiting.
- Look at all three Cs: someone with capability, competence, and communication skills can be very valuable.
- If you don't have the right people in the right places, most work on processes and strategy is a waste of time.
- The right people will figure things out but that is no excuse for not being diligent about strategy, roles, processes, and communication.

In essence, I have continued to use RO and reap the benefits. Actually, whenever I take an assignment, one prerequisite is that of getting an agreement that I can use the principles and methodologies of RO. The main reasons are that I have found it to be a competitive advantage and that it helps me towards realising a vision of improving people's daily life in the jungle of the organisational complex—big or small. Everyone deserves to have a great manager that shows a broader perspective, a clear delegation of tasks, and company that helps gradually growing his/her challenges and work in line with the person's inner potential.

Author's Note: Consider how this case study fits the sequence of events for building an organisation.

The sequence of events is listed below:

1. *Decide where we are going—*
2. *Determine how we are going to get there.*
3. *Decide how we will organise ourselves*
4. *Decide what works needs to be done.*
5. *Decide how roles are related and ensure authority matches accountability.*
6. *Recruit and deploy people.*
7. *Ensure coherence through Managerial Leadership.*

Case Study 2

The Road Ahead: The Royal Automobile Association (RAA) of South Australia (2007-2012)

This is an update of the case study presented at the Third Biennial World Conference of the Global Organisation Society in Buenos Aires, 2009, by Andrew Olivier and Ian Stone, CEO of RAA. This case study follows the sequence of events and the seven principles.

Background

The Royal Automobile Association (RAA) is a Southern Australian icon which since 1903 has been serving its members in providing roadside assistance, travel information, and more lately insurance. The Association, with more than half a million members (representing more people than any other organisation, outside State Parliament), liaises with state government bodies and plays an advisory and advocacy role on their behalf. It is a member of a global association of motoring clubs.

In 2007, Ian Stone was appointed the fifth CEO in its 105-year history. Ian wanted to reposition the organisation and refresh its strategies, structures, systems, and the way it managed its people. Ian had been introduced to the ideas of Elliott Jaques when he headed up the RAA Insurance Company and wanted to introduce the same concepts and leadership principles in RAA.

The Organisation Renewal Intervention (August 2007-December 2012)

The Executive Team

The 2007 period started with a change to the executive team as new general managers were appointed in finance, sales and marketing, and IS. The other divisional areas of operations, public affairs, and human resources remained unchanged, except upgrading the HR manager's position to general management. An external consultant was appointed to assist the project as adviser.

Current capability and future potential were all key aspects of general manager selection, and the new CEO set about building himself a competent team of high-potential individuals. He had great plans for the future.

The Strategy

Automotive clubs around the world are built on a strong foundation of responding to people in need. For multiple decades, in some cases more than a century, they have provided the answer to one of the motorists biggest concerns—that their car will break down, and they won't know how to fix it.

Providing such a valued service has been reflected in the internal culture of motoring clubs, which are often considered to be wonderful working environments with many lifelong friends made the atmosphere that resembles a large family company. Many of its1,000 employees having served for twenty years plus. The average period of service is twelve years.

At the same time, the world was entering a global financial crises, and the transport industry would be facing its toughest ever challenge as traditional models of transport came under scrutiny with global warming.

The new CEO led a scenario-planning session to create a ten-year strategic plan, based on different scenarios. This strategic plan called for an overhaul of the business, its structures, its people strategies, systems, and the move towards an entrepreneurial performance-based culture. To enable this, a long-term Organisational Renewal (OR) plan was put in place.

The need is to maintain costs, and, in some markets, competition also created the need for more long-term focus and diversification. The need for efficient operations and other profitable businesses has never been higher, but this requires strategies and execution that now takes place over a number of years.

The new strategy had a number of moving parts, dealing with not only the ongoing core of the business, the 24 × 7 roadside emergency service but also with understanding their membership base better. This was translated into offering allied services with deeper penetration and increased product uptake. New exciting entrepreneurial ventures were also to be identified. The strategy was fully endorsed by a very active board, and the RAA was firmly placed on a new growth strategy which allowed for diversification.

The OR project has played a key role in ensuring alignment of accountabilities around this shared objective which will be achieved this financial year.

In 2009, the RAA bought its JV insurance company from its partner, Suncorp Insurance. This purchase entailed developing a software system to replace the previously shared back-end system. Executive leadership saw significant growth and synergy opportunities, and what ensued was a three-year project that cut across functional divisions and product silos. The new system promised integration and growth opportunities and was successfully activated in early 2012.

This project was a full 'hinge level project' operating in work level IV, and once in place and 'bedded down', it would become part of normal work level III practices. As a project, it represented a radical departure from the 'normal' way of doing business and called for process redesign, changed ways of working, and changed role authority and accountabilities across many parts of the organisation. Products, sales, membership, marketing, product training, finance, claims, and underwriting were all impacted and were in essence rewired. While the constraints of resources and budget do not allow for the project to be 100 per cent requisite, being able to identify areas where issues may occur and having a framework for discussion has been found to be extremely valuable.

The insurance company had started the same OR project earlier, in 2005, but with changes in CEO, only part of the organisation remained requisite by 2009.

The ten-year RAA strategic plan has over the past four years moved the organisation forward. When the project commenced in 2007, leadership scans across the organisation gave it an aggregated risk profile of 2.8 which meant it was at risk of delivering on its strategic intent). In April 2012, a similar exercise was repeated, with the organisation achieving a score of 3.2, indicating it was 'requisite'.

Enabling this has been a structure with the requisite number of levels to achieve the strategy, clear accountabilities, and authorities at each work level. This has been possible because of having clarity on the Strategic Intent.

Four years after agreement on the intent, all the financial targets for the ten-year plan had been achieved. This was as a result of the purchase of the insurance company. The computer systems project which resulted was the largest single project undertaken by the RAA.

In addition to this, since the adoption of the Strategic Intent, general managers at work level IV have delivered on the following during this period:

- Returning the operations of the business to profit. Since this strategy meeting reliance on investment markets for ongoing financial sustainability has been eliminated and operational expenses have been reduced as additional revenue sources have been gained.
- The first refresh of the brand in thirty-five years.
- Clear identification of four 'product pillars' to clarify the offerings for members.
- Movement beyond motoring into the wider field of 'mobility' to support the changing needs of members.

- Strategic repositioning of the smaller businesses of travel and security.
- Revamping and updating of the distribution network across the state.
- Four acquisitions of smaller organisations that aligned with the strategic intent of the business
- The capability in place to run the programme of implementing the new system referred to above with internal resources, supported by external expertise as required.

Understanding the Talent Pool and People Day

(Principle 6: Matching Individual Capability to Role Complexity)

From 2007 onwards, the entire talent pool was mapped through two processes—capability interviews and the process called Rapid Talent Pool Evaluation (RTPe). This exercise, which relies heavily on the manager and MoR process was done for all departments.

Each department with its general manager went through a structured exercise to understand its human capital and the opportunities and vulnerabilities. The outcome of each exercise was fed into a People Day, when the CEO and his executive team review talent. The first People Day happened in November 2008 and was the first exercise of its kind to provide a bird's-eye view of human capital. The People Day is now held annually and plays a significant role in talent management. It is based on the MoR system.

Ian Stone, CEO says,

'The People Day process gave me and my executive team our first all-encompassing view of who we had in our organisation, and what they would be capable of in the future. Doing this as a team gave us consistency across the entire business, and it has been a critical process not just in identifying talent, but in putting peer pressure onto the team to ensure poor performers are addressed. As we have become more familiar with the process, the value of the sessions continue to go even higher with looking for opportunities and discussing movement of high-potential staff now commonplace amongst my team. It has been a bit plus for staff

as well, knowing that their manager's manager is watching out for their career and that their particular path is discussed at the highest level.'

Part of the RTPe process involves looking at structure from a levels-of-work perspective. The RTPe process provided a solid return in terms of being a relatively quick way of *assessing people and structure* with full managerial support and input.

The MoR Review and Performance Management

The performance system called the Continuous Development Process (CDP) is an annual cycle and was upgraded with the introduction of the MoR review. The CEO performed this with his skip-level reports, the GMs, and managers with theirs.

The CDP as a result of these and other performance-related changes have been upgraded and migrated to an online environment. Performance information is now added into individual data for the People Day sessions, which will be held annually. All employees are aware of and now understand the function of a MoR.

While the manager answers the question, 'How am I doing?', many employees regard the MoR interview as the single most tangible and useful outcome of the OD exercise as it allow them to have another view on that fourth question—*'What's my future?'*

Organisational Pulse

Numerous leadership scans, levels of work reviews, and capability maps were prepared as benchmarks and to be clear where focus would deliver the best outcomes. Leadership scans identified common themes across the organisation, such as the need for

- *improved tasking.*
- *performance-driven outcomes.*
- *resolving unclear roles—work levels were compromised with key roles spanning two or more levels.*
- *resolving unclear authority and accountability.*

In 2010, an organisation-wide survey was conducted, which reflected a number of hotspot areas that could be linked back to the earlier leadership scans. Some areas showed significant improvement, such as authority and accountability and improved tasking. Of interest was a relatively low score in communication despite a number of initiatives in place to improve the flow of information from the executive team through to the front-line staff. At the same time, scores for areas such as understanding future direction and knowing my own job showed significant improvement.

This suggested that the work of the executive team in providing clarity about their own areas and its work had been successful as clear levels of work and accountability/authority were put in place. It also showed that the next stage of development is creating an environment which allows for more natural flow of information between areas, as the communication referred to by staff in the survey was often regarding other areas of the organisation.

A focus on cross-functional role types and their authorities was agreed as the next area of development.

Leadership Practices

(Principle 7: Ensuring Leadership Coherence)

In October 2008, the general managers with the CEO undertook an *Organisation and Leadership Effectiveness Programme*. Throughout the rest of 2008 and 2009, this process was cascaded into each department with the respective general managers leading the workshop with the external advisor as facilitator.

The process involved the departmental head—departments are based on the three-tier building block led by work level IV general managers *(Principle 2)* working with the external facilitator to provide incumbents with an induction into the Managerial Leadership competencies required for work level III. The workshop linked these competencies back to the general, manager's business plan. Prior to each workshop, the facilitator and GM worked together preparing for the workshop, and throughout the event, the principles were linked to real business issues and workplace behaviours to illustrate the learning.

Each department was surveyed on their strengths and vulnerabilities using a leadership scan before the workshop. In some cases, the scan involved a levels-of-work review and a capability map.

Leadership practices were rolled out to work level II Front-Line Managers and specialist from 2009. A one-and-a-half day induction was followed up with projects that were undertaken by delegates to investigate how requisite were different practices were around the organisation.

The projects required a ten-minute presentation to their manager and MoR (sometimes with the CEO in attendance). The first set of presentations were a mixed bag, with some aspects given below, clearly indicating that the delegates' managers had not engaged in the project, while some were outstanding and added to ensuring requisite practices. Examples of project topics were as follows:

- Cross-functional role authorities
- Marketing department restructure
- Performance feedback

Infrastructure Support

The OD team plus selected line managers were trained in levels of work analysis and in understanding the framework for support and training. The aim was to ensure all Managerial Leaders understood enough about structure to ensure that PDs were based on time spans and UVAs, and all had clear authority and accountabilities spelled out. This venture was not as successful as hoped, since the once-off induction workshop was not sufficient to ensure widespread knowledge.

What was very successful was the understanding of role authority and the different role types (TIRR and TARR) and the MoR review of the performance management system for individual effectiveness.

In 2012, a programme to refresh managerial leaders on the principles of effective design will be undertaken.

Induction and Communication

Induction programmes were upgraded to include a talk by a GM with a DVD of the CEO and senior managers talking about requisite practices and the RAA. In 2011, dedicated HR specialists were appointed to support the organisation and to assist delivery on the 2012-2015-OD plan. The Intranet and iConnect features information on the OD project with support and help. 2012 saw a drive focusing on the accountability of Managerial Leaders for comprehensive induction.

Recruitment and PDs

The online system to support the agreed recruitment requirements for role and individual has been developed. It provides an online template and guide and will serve as an organisational database for storage of interactive PDs which reflect the following:

- Authority linked to accountabilities.
- Role type.
- Level of work defined through UVA.
- Time span of decision-making.
- Systems and processes which impact the role and related authorities.
- Training internal recruitment consultants in the use of a tool called IRIS to assist in matching capability to role complexity.

Restructuring

(Principle 2: Optimal Size and Principle 4: Reporting Distance)

During 2008/2009, the *Operations Department* restructured its 24/7 call centre and roadside service functions, focusing on its reporting-structure roles (Principle 4) in each level and introducing requisite authority and accountability to Front-Line Managers and managers. This was an extensive restructure and signaled the introduction of greater role accountability and authority through the elimination of non-value-adding management and supervisory layers.

Renamed Automotive Services, this division of RAA is the largest, encompassing all technical automotive products and services offered to its members. It is also responsible for the 24/7 delivery of core roadside assistance services to members and commercial clients in South Australia and Northern Territory.

RAA also operates a small niche *commercial contact centre* business using multiskilled consultants within the *RAC* to service a diverse range of clients. Following a review of the strategic direction of the organisation, a decision was taken to cull unprofitable commercial clients and refocus the *RAC* on its core business.

Although the *Automotive Services* work group is comprised of a loyal and dedicated management team that understands the primary business and has the skills to successfully manage the day-to-day activities of delivering excellent outcomes, there was a lack of capacity and capability to meet the challenges of a changing external and internal environment.

After introducing the OR concepts and principles during the Leadership Framework programme, a series of management workshops were undertaken to review the nature of work being undertaken across the main workgroups and apply the Leadership Framework principles in establishing appropriate roles and structures. Authority and accountabilities were set to match the role type (aligned with vertical and cross-functional role relationships). Clear business purposes and context for each role was defined. The restructuring sought to create clearer role accountabilities with increased authority, allowing removal of non-value adding activity and excessive supervisory and managerial layers.

Figure 18a and 18b shows the old and new structure of Road Services while Figure 18c and 18d the old and new structure for the Operations Assistance Centre. The reduction in pseudo work levels is clear.

Figure 18a: **Old structure of road service (six levels)**

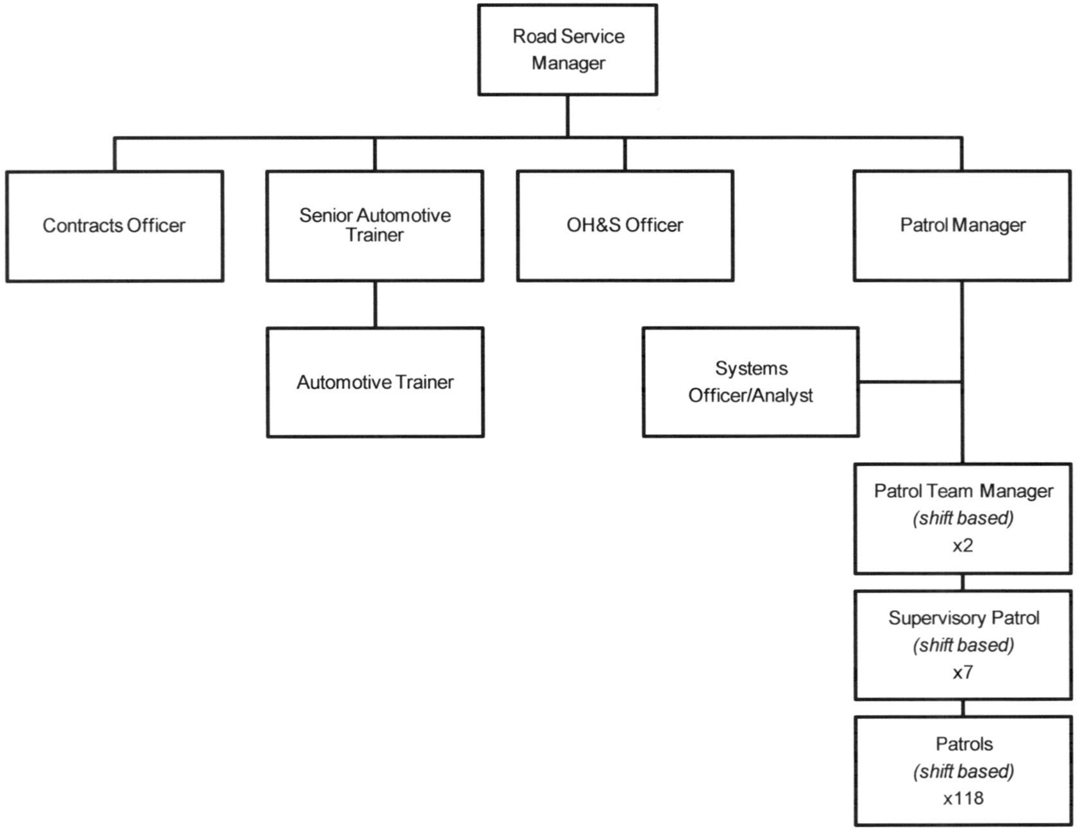

Figure 18b: **New Structure of Road Service (three levels)**

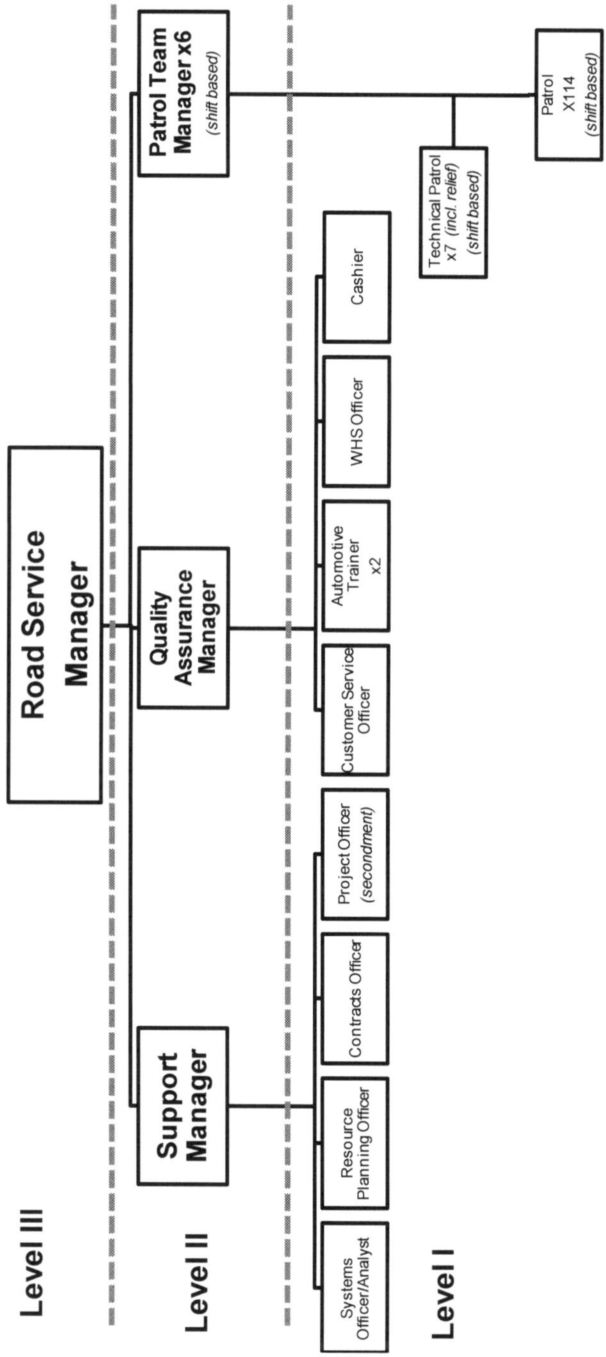

Figure 18c: **Old Structure of Roadside Assistance Centre (five levels)**

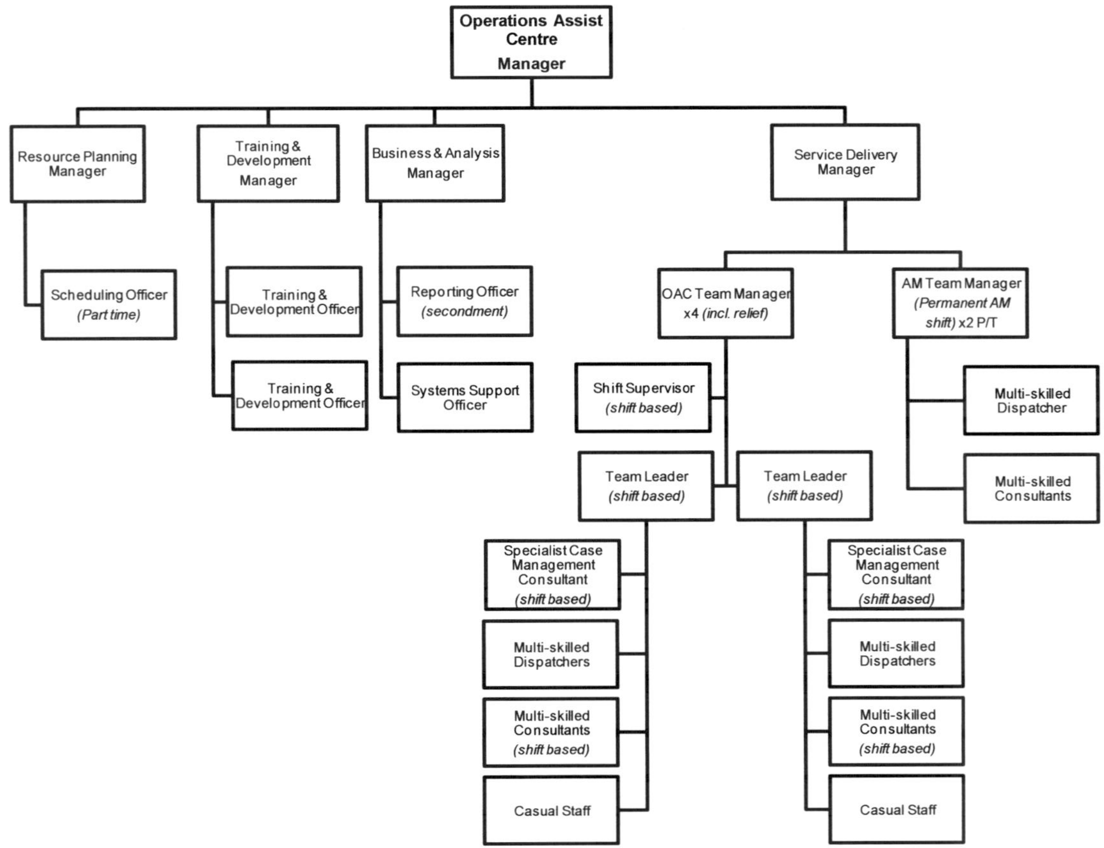

Figure 18d: **New Structure of Operations Assistance Centre (three levels)**

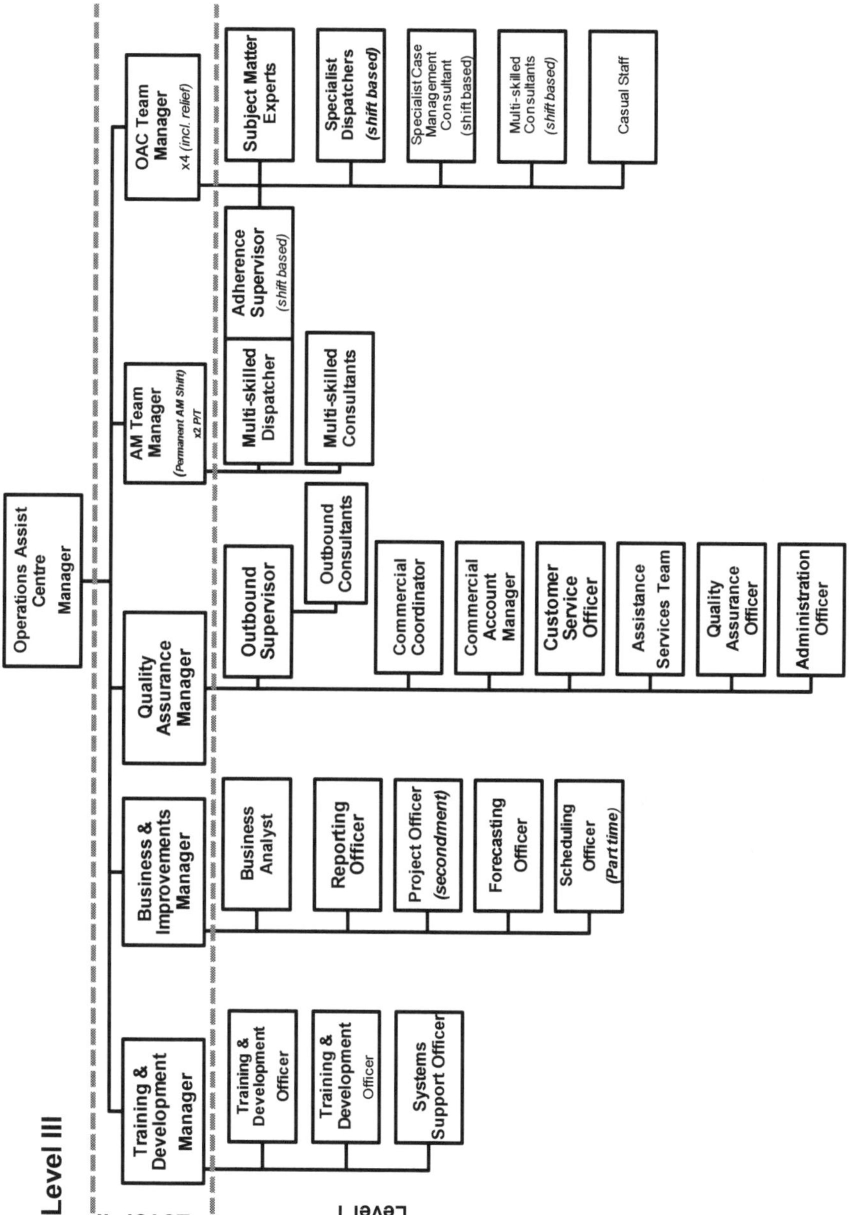

After a couple of years of bedding down the new *Automotive Services* structure, it became clear that several of the incumbents were unable or unwilling to operate effectively at the required level and further structural refinements were instigated to address the issues and foster greater collaboration and consistency across the large work groups.

All common support activities within the RAC and Road Service work groups (e.g. systems, forecasting, resource planning, analysis, and reporting) were centralised under a new senior manager, and a new level III strategy role was created to aid the general manager in fostering longer term initiatives and execution of major projects. This created an opportunity of injecting new senior management talent with recruitment and selection a pivotal part in ensuring appropriate capability was secured.

The new team and structure has continued to oversee the delivery of exceptional service to RAA members but has also positioned the business unit to embark on a major business system transformational project commencing in 2012/2013. The two-to-three year project will see the complete replacement of core systems used in the delivery of 24/7 roadside assistance, using technological advancements to automate roadside transactions and processes, eliminate paper-based transactions, and broaden the methods used by members to request RAA assistance.

A new general manager of *Information Services* commenced in November 2010, providing opportunity for a thorough review of structure to support the 2018 Strategic Intent. It was identified that the business required level III management across three functions—software development, infrastructure, and the new area of planning and architecture. This third area was previously mixed in with the other two roles, leading to a lack of resourcing in the crucial areas of working with the business on their future plans and communicating these needs back to both software and infrastructure.

Additional resources were also brought in at high level II to manage relationships with commercial software providers to ensure that the large amount of experience in in-house development was supplemented with management skill of external relationships.

Sales and Marketing[67]*:* During the 2008 scans of the organisation, only one department within RAA was found to have a requisite structure. This was the Retail Distribution sales force that is located within the Sales and Marketing Department. Being a sales division, there was a strong natural requisite structure with front-line salespeople and supervisors focussed on the Quality work theme (work level I) and the transactional regional and Contact Centre Managers at the Service work theme (work level II) and a single senior manager at Practice (work level III). He in turn reported to a general manager at work level IV.

During 2011, the structure of the business was reviewed. The outcome showed that while the division remained mostly requisite, there were some areas that required attention. Most of the changes made were around the areas of authority and accountability for daily operations and consolidating this in the hands of Sales Team Manager in each front-line team and the streamlining of processes to serve the member by clarification of cross-functional and specialist TIRR roles. As a result of the scan, changes have meant that the Retail Call Centre (RCC) is now entirely focussed on the member and achieving their sales results while being requisite.

The final change was within the Retail Operations Team. In the past, the team was responsible for a mixture of department-wide support and product silos. With the restructure occurring in the RCC, there was an opportunity to also restructure this team and to create a vacancy for talent-pool management.

Another factor in this restructure was moving all silo activity from this team so that they would only work on cross-functional activity. In part, this was in preparation for the deployment of the new IT system for the group (as a result of the purchase of the Insurance Company). Activity in web and shop buying were moved out of the team with activity in product training and help desk now complementing business improvement, reporting, and sales training within the Retail Operations Team. So not only is the structure requisite but so is their activity as a team.

What this demonstrates is that while a division can be naturally requisite, there is a need to review this structure from time to time, question some of the roles, and align work to the primary intent of the organisation.

A strategy and investments department was set up to investigate *new business development* opportunities and moribund parts of the existing business were focused on for rejuvenation. A number of opportunities were investigated, allowing the organisation to further test its own strategic intent while building capability in work of this nature. Clear accountabilities has led to a strong team at work level IV (a hinge-level project) across investments, strategy, market development, public affairs, and commercial business all being active in shaping new opportunities and identifying which ones to proceed to level III analysis of feasibility and implementation.

RAA Secure Services: The RAA security business was initially placed under the strategy and investments area to ensure focus on its strategic development and to better integrate across the organisation (the key competitive advantage in its markets).

The business provides home security and personal alarms to members, general consumers, and for commercial purposes. Commencing in 1994, it has grown to a multimillion-dollar-turnover business through the dedication of its manager and loyal staff. The same manager continues to work in the business today. Reporting structures of the business had seen it passed between general managers as there was no obvious place for it to reside.

The previous three years had seen a noticeable plateau in terms of business growth, and attempts to generate additional business through increased marketing did not have expected effects. Acknowledging that the business was operating well below its potential, accountability for the business was given to young manager transitioning into work level IV who was employed in the new strategy and investments area.

In addition, the Marketing Department assigned responsibility for the marketing and distribution of the security business to a newly hired work level III product development manager. *Thus the organisation was able, through its new systems, to understand its talent pool and to deploy its human capital in line with its organisational needs and critically focus high-potential individuals into growth areas.*

An analysis using RO principles uncovered the following:

- The business needed to be managed at work level III and led at IV.
- Level II Front-Line Management was problematic, resulting in the manager being forced to operate at too low a level, thus leaving a levels-of-work gap.
- Linkages to other areas in the organisation suffered as plans were not able to be made and seen through, for example, marketing.
- Role authorities lacked definition.
- Overall purpose of the business was not clearly articulated along with clear goals to be achieved.

From December 2008, these issues were addressed using the budgeting and planning cycle as the catalyst. A clear profit objective was agreed upon and plans were put into place with immediate results seen in terms of marketing and distribution with a 40 per cent increase in bottom-line performance.

With the ability to gain market share now proven, a restructure was required in order to ensure that growth could be managed without service levels decreasing and staff being asked to work under an unfair level of stress. Level III management of the business was divided into three areas with the founder of the business, a natural entrepreneur and dealmaker, given accountability for locating and making acquisitions to consolidate the market. This relieved him of the level III burden of continuous operational improvement which was given to a young manager working below capability at level II. In addition, a veteran of the industry who had been restrained at level II under the previous structure was also given level III responsibility for the other operational side of the business.

The restructure has seen the acquisition strategy become business as usual, while the business is now has 40 per cent more customers than three years ago. Service levels and staff morale is at high levels, and the growth plans envisaged in 2008 can now occur in a structure which is sustainable. Importantly, the three level III managers have taken full accountability for the business in meeting and improving on the needs of current markets, allowing the level IV manager to concentrate on the strategic development of the business. This is expected to lead to new areas of opportunity for the organisation as a whole.

2012-2015

In 2011, a renewed business plan for organisational effectiveness was approved by the CEO with a number of identified key initiatives and desired outcomes. Two TIRR roles with appropriate authority were established to coordinate, monitor, and provide advisory services.

Authors Note: In case study 2, identify where and how the seven principles for designing organizational structure were applied.

Principle 1: Business Intent—Required Complexity

How many work levels were needed to deliver the organisation's purpose?

Principle 2: Optimal Size

There is a design blueprint for all functions that starts with the team, which has a scalable three-tier structure. How was this applied?

Principle 3: Making Decisions equals Work

By analysing the tasks and time span, one can understand the work level. What examples of this can you find?

Principle 4: Reporting Distance

One role must not report to another in the same level of work to avoid duplications and overlaps. This was followed in the restructuring exercises to what effect?

Principle 5: Empowering Role Relationships

Understanding role types and their authority is important as it empowers structure and processes horizontally. Was this regarded as important?

Principle 6: Matching Individual Capability to Role Complexity

Appoint people to the role who can handle the level of work complexity. An individual appointed into a role must have the current actual capability at that given point in time to carry out the level of work complexity required. Where did this process start? What was one of the first things the new CEO did?

Principle 7: Ensuring Leadership Coherence

Everyday practices needs to ensure that work is taking place at the right level for driving outcomes. Ensure coherence through managerial competence to apply these principles using a common language of understanding. How was this principle dealt with and how effective was it?

Case Study 3

Integration of Two Latin American Mining Services Companies

This case study was supplied by AMG Consulting, Argentina. It is a classic tale of growth based on the resource boom. The case study is different from the previous case studies in that it has as yet no long-term outcomes to present, and secondly, it is not a standalone business but deals with a friendly merger of two independent organisations. Observe how the sequence of events and seven principles are applied in the two phases of organisational design.

This case describes the creation of a new organisation designed to implement an aggressive growth strategy in Latin America and, ultimately, on a global scale. It presents unique challenges across four connected fronts:

- To achieve the goals of shareholders from two countries with a history of geopolitical tension.
- The simultaneous implementation of a competitive strategy in two time horizons.
- The structural design of a Requisite Organisation for achieving medium and the long-term strategic objectives
- And the balanced integration of the leadership teams of both companies.
- Critical for the successful implementation of a Requisite Orgnisation were the alignment with the business model and

strategy on processes, roles, accountabilities, and authorities plus the involvement of key stakeholders throughout the project.

Background

The economic growth experienced by Latin America in the last decade stands in stark contrast to the recurring crises that historically plagued the entire region. As an *emerging economy*, Latin America presents a context of opportunity, mainly tied to the production of raw materials and the exploitation of natural resources. At the same time, a growing middle class, which in 2010 counted 382 million potential consumers, represents a significant and attractive market not only for multinational companies from developed countries, but also for a new class of international enterprise—the *Multilatinas*, regional companies that expand beyond the borders of their country of origin to aggressively compete in the global economy.

The mining industry is one of the economic sectors with the greatest growth fueled by increasing demand and record prices. In the next decade, Chile, Peru, Mexico, and Brazil are expected to attract multibillion-dollar investments for the exploration and exploitation of minerals. It is within this context that two companies based in Latin America decided to explore ways to create a strategic alliance.

Company I, based in Peru, is a leader in manufacturing for the mining industry. It holds 60 per cent market share in underground mining and 17 per cent in open-pit mining and exports its products to the United States, Canada, Chile, Ecuador, and Bolivia.

Company II, mainly a service company based in Chile, also manufactures mining supplies. It is recognised as one of the most important players in the Latin American industry.

Initially, the companies forged a commercial agreement to market complementary products throughout Latin America. However, the longer term objective was to have operational and legal integration in order to offer comprehensive services, capture synergies, and project a market presence that could allow them to become the leading provider of mining services on a global scale. Their plan is to first achieve regional pre-eminence in five years in the mining markets of Chile, Peru, Argentina, Panama, Colombia, Brazil, and Mexico, and then expand to other regions in seven to ten years.

The major shareholders designated a top executive from each company (one the future CEO) to head a team tasked with exploring the feasibility of the intended alliance and to define the business model and strategy. The team was also to design the regional organisation required to successfully execute the business plan. The vision and determination of the future CEO was to be a critical success factor.

A consulting company was retained to assist, and the consulting engagement was structured in two phases.

Phase I: Strategy Definition and Organisational Design

It included restatement of the business model and definition of the value proposition and strategy that will ensure competitive differentiation and design in order to grow the business in the transition, and the definition of roles and accountabilities to ensure effective execution.

Phase II: Organisational Implementation and Cultural Integration

This involved the development of Managerial Leadership practices, assistance in the transition to assume new roles and accountabilities, and the integration of national and business cultures within the organisation (*Principle 7*).

The following description refers to the implementation of phase I and follows the sequence of events described below.

A. Vision and Strategy: A Radical Shift in the Business Model

The objective was *to formulate a shared vision with specific goals for the long-term, define a business model that clearly established a strategy for competitive differentiation, and to establish criteria to facilitate the design of the Requisite Organisation.*

The greatest difficulty in this phase was that the two co-leaders of the project had a personal stake in its outcome, and they were operating under instructions to protect and enhance the interests of the shareholders that each one represented. There was also uncertainty regarding the nature, extent, and strategy for the intended alliance.

The consultants followed two guidelines in the design of this phase of the engagement: (a) due to the short time available to prepare for the integration of both companies, the process had to be well structured in order to produce relevant, well-founded, and efficient discussions; (b) to create an environment that would promote frank exchanges, thus building the necessary trust to ensure a successful integration.

The engagement entailed the following:

- Strategic review of the business context (economic trends, markets, demand, competition, etc.) in which the intended alliance would operate.
- In-depth discussion to clarify and agree on a shared vision, including specific goals and their time spans. Definition of the value proposition to ensure competitive differentiation and the organisational capabilities required for execution.
- Determination of the level of complexity for the business strategy and its implications in terms of organisational design and required human capability.
- Definition of organisational design guidelines consistent with RO principles and functional to the realities of both companies.

Key management personnel from both companies participated throughout the process. Frequent group discussions eased the airing of differences, facilitated the creation of consensus, improved trust, and helped to eliminate unfounded fears.

A significant outcome of this process was a major change in the core business, where the value proposition shifted from a *product focus* to a *solutions focus*. This shift also implied changes in the business model, the underlying processes, as well as in the organisational and individual capabilities that were critical for a successful implementation. The nature of the questions shifted from how to why?

Mission

'To contribute to the safe and efficient use of resources by our customers for their productive processes and in the growth of their business.'

Value Proposition

Customised solutions for the exploitation of mining resources up to the reduction and refining plants.

Design, supply, and implementation of process management systems to improve productivity and profitability of capital employed in the productive processes.

Joint management of risks and benefits resulting from relevant processes and accruing to stakeholders.

Vision

To become a world-class company in the supply of innovative and efficient solutions for the . . . (*omitted due to confidentiality*)

To be the leader in Latin America (five years), and one of the three top companies in the world (in seven to ten years) in the supply of products and services to the mining industry.

To be perceived by our clients as strategic partners contributing to the sustainable and profitable growth of their business.

To be a global, innovative, customer-centred company with strong local presence and cultural affinity with our customers.

To be one organisation with one culture: trustworthy, safe, simple, and efficient, and with the best people.

B. Major Increase in the Level of Complexity

The scope of the vision implied a major increase in the level of complexity, specifically the move to work level V in the short term and work level VI in the long term.

The increased complexity is due to the following:

1. **Globalisation of Demand/Concentration of Purchasing Power of Customers**
   A trend is towards consolidation in the mining industry and the reduction in the number of supply contracts that are more global in scope, increasing the negotiating power of customers.
   While companies I and II separately had a marketing approach and supply processes directed to customers' contacts in work levels III and IV, the new value proposition and the globalisation of demand require interaction with customers' management at level V or higher.

2. **Growth Objectives**
   The business is expected to grow from a dominant position in the local markets of Chile and Peru and limited presence in other Latin American countries to a position of regional leadership in the span of five years and global leadership in ten years.
   This strategy contemplates organic growth in established markets, alliances, mergers, and the opening of new markets; all of which involve decisions with a longer time span.

3. **Major Shift in the Value Proposition**

- Develop and install processes and practices to support the new business model.
- Convert the transactional relationship with customers into a more permanent bond with the company becoming an integral part of the value chain of its customers.
- Promote an organisational culture focused on developing critical skills to ensure competitive differentiation.
- Attract, recruit, and retain human capital required to successfully compete on a global scale.

Ensure Sustainable Competitive Advantages

The delivery of innovative solutions requires profound knowledge of the customer processes, practices, and values, and to work effectively with and within its organisation.

In the case of the mining industry, the sustainability of the business depends to great extent on the careful management of stakeholders' relations; government, national, and international regulations; local communities; public opinion; and so on.

4. **Blending of Diverse Organisational Cultures**
   The vision and strategies required the development of a new organisational culture with common values, processes, and practices and effectively blending the organisations.

C. Organisational Design Guidelines

The in-depth analysis of the above factors increased the management's understanding of the main concepts behind Elliott Jaques's Requisite Organisation such as the complexity inherent to a task, the level of complexity implicit in a business strategy, the relationship between time span and complexity, and the number of distinct managerial levels appropriate to execute the strategy at various stages of the project.

To complement the general principles, specific criteria was develop to address the timing, reality, and business nature of the company.

The general principles used were

- The business strategy defines the maximum level of complexity to be managed by the organisation.(Principle 1)
- From this definition emanate the authority and accountability of the CEO and the requisite number of managerial levels for the organisation. (Principle 2)
- The ideal distance between the levels of complexity assigned to manager and subordinate is one stratum.(Principle 4)
- The organisational complexity should be managed, not reduced or eliminated. RO calls for a structure that seeks simplicity and effectiveness through the following:

  - ☐ Definition of key processes to execute the business strategy. (Principles 3 & 5)
  - ☐ Clear assignment of accountabilities for every role including cross-functional interactions. (Principle 5)

- ☐ Allocation of human capability consistent with the level of complexity inherent to each role. (Principle 6)

- The successful implementation of RO demands *leadership* that sets the *strategic direction* for the business, manages the required *organisational capabilities,* maximises *individual contributions*, and models essential *values and culture* for the entire organisation. (Principle 7)

The specific application of these criteria was the creation of a corporate office to *articulate the interests of the two shareholders, to define and lead the international growth, and to facilitate the capture of synergies*. Such corporate office was to add tangible value, acting with speed, flexibility, and world-class quality.

The creation of a role at the corporate level was dictated by

- the relevance of the processes involved to sustain the business model and the value proposition, the need to project a corporate brand on a global scale,
- the importance of capturing operating synergies,
- to ensure the standardisation and application of policies and practices that are key to the sustainability of the business, and
- to seek growth opportunities in a coordinated manner.

At the country level (local operating units):

- Local management was to be accountable for the administration and results of the areas assigned to each country.
- Certain functions were to remain at the local level: sales and customer service, accounting and administration, regulatory compliance, safety-quality-environmental issues, and community relations.

D. Present Situation

Both, companies operated in their parent countries through a level IV organisation. Both companies managed, in addition, certain local operations and the export business to countries with no local presence.

A diagnostic review identified the following organisational dysfunctions that needed attention in the new integrated structure.

Organisational Dysfunctions—Company I

- Excessive divisions in the management of production areas.
- Unclear definition of accountabilities for quality, safety, and environmental issues between operating and support functions and for planning issues between administration and systems/processes.
- Levels of complexity of several functions in the commercial area were not properly identified.
- The delivery of mining services (an operating activity) was under the supervision of the commercial area.

Organisational Dysfunctions—Company II

- Unclear definition and assignment of accountability for technical development between the commercial and the engineering functions.
- Unclear definition of interactions between the management of line and support functions (human resources, safety, and environment).
- Two maintenance areas with limited coordination.

E. Organisational Design of the Corporate Office

The design of the new organisation contemplated a transitional stage to conduct the regional expansion in the medium term, and a long-term design to support the strategy of global expansion. In both cases, the roles assigned to the corporate office seek to strengthen the position of the company in their countries of origin, capture synergies (operations, supply chain, exports, and R&D), conduct a consolidated strategy of investment and growth, homogenise policies, standards and practices, develop a corporate strategy of market positioning and branding, and coordinate the supply and servicing of export markets. See Figure 19a

Corporate Office (Requisite Structure)

The recommended design presents a work-level gap between the CEO and the functions of R&D, human capital, safety, and environment because the projected growth resulting from the company's long-term strategy does not warrant a full-blown level VI organisation.

Corporate Office (Transition Organisation)

Due to the two-step nature of the growth strategy spelled out in the company's vision, a transition organisation was designed for the corporate office to reflect the level of complexity of the shorter time horizon and to focus on the major challenges of this phase.

During the transition, the two main countries required to be directly managed by a level V executive due their importance as a platform for growth and relevance for business results.

Figure 19 a: **Transition Structure of Corporate Office**

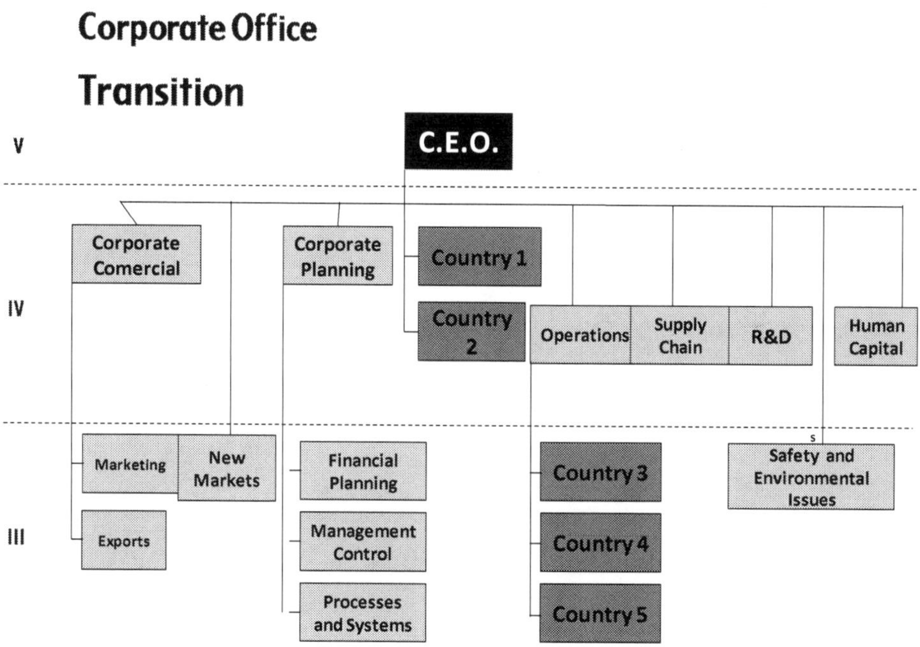

F. Organisational Design of Local Units (Country Organisations)

- Country organisations with the general manager positioned at work level IV assume overall accountability for execution of business strategy and delivery of results for the areas under their management. See Figure 19b.
- Local operations produce to satisfy demand under their responsibility and within their manufacturing capabilities. Other market needs are coordinated and satisfied through the corporate export function.
- Overall strategic direction and investment plans emanate from the corporate office. However, effective discharge of assigned responsibilities requires the articulation of market and operational variables at the local level. Functional areas are headed up with managers at work level III.

Figure 19b: **Organisational structure of each country**

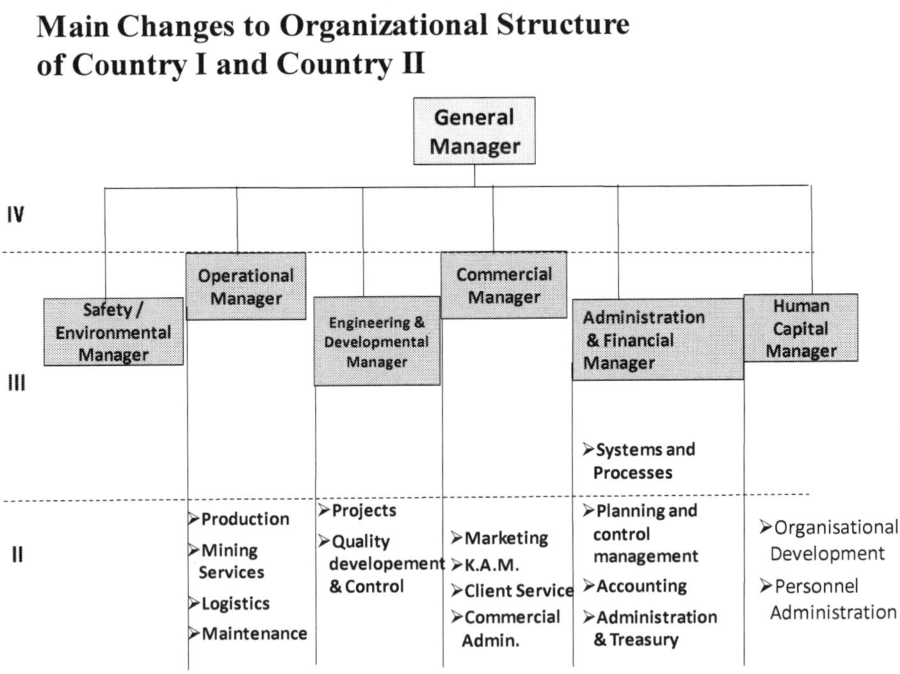

G. Definition of Accountabilities

The functions were defined for a total of forty-five managerial roles at the corporate and local unit levels.

H. Talent Evaluation, Human Capability Survey, and Coverage Strategy

Having the 'right' people in the 'right' job is a critical organsational principle. In this particular case, in addition to evaluating human capability of the managerial ranks and assessing its consistency with the level of complexity of each role, the engagement required dealing with political variables that could influence the decision-making process.

The shareholders of company I and company II sought an objective, expert recommendation on the actual and potential capability of the possible occupants of the positions in the integrated organisation.

The consultants proposed a methodology that combined the judgment of the direct superior, the professional assessment of expert consultants, and the input of an evaluation committee made up of senior members of the project team. The assessment segment had also a feedback and professional development component. *MoR inputs was not possible at this stage of transition.*

A total of forty executives were interviewed and a human capability map was created, contrasting it to the talent needs of the transitional and the long-term organisations. The Capability Map revealed a clear deficit, especially in critical roles of planning and marketing. The situation grew worse when human capability was projected five years out, particularly in light of the increase to level VI in the complexity of the strategy, the creation of a corporate office to lead the integrated business, and the retirement of several top executives.

While it was possible to assume that future acquisitions and alliances may bring additional resources, the global demand for talent in the industry required to implement a two-pronged attack to solve the shortage through internal development of the talent pipeline and the recruitment of external talent. Estimated payroll costs for the new organisation were also presented for the approval to the shareholders of both companies.

I. Conclusions and Recommendations

The following priorities were recommended:

Priorities of Strategy

- Consolidate leading market positions in Chile and Peru and enter the Brazilian market.
- Capitalise on the operational synergies offered by the current businesses.
- Accelerate the development of new solutions (competitive differentiation).
- Promote the shift of the value proposition at all levels of the organisation.
- Deepen the understanding of the evolution of markets and the industry in order to develop a sustainable and profitable strategy for long term.

Organisational Priorities

- Validate and implement recommendations for the transitional organisation.
- Constitute the transition team in alignment with the transitional organisation.
- Implement recommended changes in the structures of Chile and Peru, consistent with recommendations for the RO.

Human Capital Priorities

- Cover talent shortages in the critical roles of the corporate office, following recommendations emanating from the analysis of the talent map, validated with the project leadership.
- Recruit to cover local vacancies created by the staffing of the corporate office with internal talent.
- Design and implement a talent pipeline process to satisfy the needs generated by the strategy of growth, to promote a high-performance culture, and to strengthen organisational commitment.

Results

The main results emanating from the first phase of the project were the following:

1. Consensus on the vision, business model, and value proposition to build a distinctive competitive advantage at the regional and global levels.
2. In-depth understanding of the organisational and human capability implications of proposed strategic goals.
3. Preparedness of executives to tackle the transition to the integrated company.
4. Clarity as to the role of the future CEO of the new organisation and the nature and scope of his leadership during the transition.
5. Design of a transitory organisation, built upon the existing realities of company I and company II with clear definition of roles and accountabilities.
6. Coverage of positions with individuals whose capability is appropriate for the demands of management of complexity of the organisational roles.
7. Comprehensive proposal to present for the approval of shareholders. The project is currently being reviewed for approval and eventual implementation.

Lessons Learned

1. It is indispensable to have a clear and shared definition of the vision, business model, and strategy in order to carry out a conscientious organisational design. Pressure for a more urgent resolution should be resisted.
2. It is more and more prevalent to have to plan and articulate strategies for several time horizons simultaneously, which requires to think of the organisation and needed capabilities from the future to the present.
3. Despite having high personal stakes in the outcome of the project, executives are capable of putting the organisational interest ahead of their own if given the opportunity and the space to deal with their fears, anxiety, and personal ambitions and to build the

necessary bridge of trust to move from the emotional plane to the rational plane.

4. The organisational design must take into account the corporate cultures and idiosyncrasies of the parts involved if it is to count on the understanding and support of those responsible for its implementation.
5. The best organisational design embraces the future and respects the past. Trade-offs between theory and reality enhance the chances of success by bringing sides together in support of a workable solution and concrete results.

Authors Note: On reading this case study consider how it adhered to the principles of organisation design and the sequence of events.

Identify the *sequence of events* in this case study:

1. *Decide where we are going* (e.g. phase I was about strategy definition and organisational structure—which principles were applied and why?).
2. *Determine how we are going to get there—(*e.g. Phase II, organisational implementation and culture integration).
3. *Decide what work needs to be done.*
4. *Decide reporting structure*—Principle 4: One role must not report to another in same work level.
5. *Decide how roles are related and ensure authority matches accountability*. (Empowering work effectively—how the system functions). Principle 5: Authority equals Accountability.
6. *Deploy people*—Deploying people to breath live into the structure. There is a principle involved. Principle 6: Match Capability to Role Complexity.
7. *Managerial Leadership*—Ensure coherence and continuity through leadership education. Principle 7: Leadership Coherence.

Conclusion

This book is aimed at explaining the seven key principles that should be used for designing effective and sustainable work structures.

It provides background to understanding work, and how the different work levels present level specific challenges, each adding value in a different way. Through applying the seven principles, the power of the team can be liberated.

The different levels of work complexity are a reality, and the models for viewing dynamic work complexity described here have evolved, have been tested, and have been refined for more than fifty years.

As Alistair Mant asserts, 'Whether one wants to ascribe to "a bold theory, which irritates some people, because it asserts the levels are immutable—it makes no difference if the organisation is a manufacturing firm, a solicitor's practice, or a diocese" it is a powerful comprehensive approach.'[68]

These models provides the know-how for structuring flexible dynamic business and for understanding work that makes complexity science so much more tangible and useable. It also plays a fundamental role in the encouragement of individual and team creativity.

For many who have been exposed to this thinking, it has created mental models about how things work that have profoundly affected them over many years. For those that have not yet been exposed, if this book stirs your interest to learn more and experiment, then it will have achieved its purpose.

I hope this handbook proves to be valuable resource to you and that it has stimulated your curiosity.

Andrew Olivier

Interested in Taking These Principles Further?

- *The Organisation Design Workshop:* This one day practical workshop is fast pace, interesting, and can be held in-house for your company's senior managers. It can be customised to address your own issues through a simple data-collection and analysis process.
- *So How Do You Match to the Seven Principles?* We offer a range of customised scanning methods to analyse your structure according to the seven principles.
- *The Effective Managerial Leadership Workshop*. This 2.5-day induction workshop is for the senior executives and their teams. It incorporates their business planning as the foundation around which the workshop is built. The workshop highlights individual development needs through an integrated set of scans linked to these principles and addresses the outcomes and business plan issues in an easy-to-follow manner, rich with case studies and examples. It is a very effective leadership development programme, and managers leave with a toolkit and a powerful mental model.

This is what clients have said about the programme.

'Andrew has provided invaluable advice and assistance to the RAA to enable to develop our talent, identify future leaders and manage our teams to maximise our output. I have used Andrew at three companies and have always got exceptional results.' (Ian Stone, CEO, RAA)

'I wanted to say thank you for the wonderful insights you provided. What I had thought intuitively around workplace structure now has a science behind it. I thoroughly enjoyed the learning and was energised by the process. It made it hard to go back to the everyday work waiting for me.' (Angela Edwards, GM Burswood Entertainment Complex)

'Andrew has brought some rigor and real depth of understanding to our business structure, management styles and future planning. He has added immense value to my role as CEO.' (Peter Blackwell, CEO, AAA Tourism, New Zealand * CTP Australia)

- **Principle 3: Capability Matches Role Complexity**. We have a number of options for assessing capability, ranging from rapid talent pool evaluation to face-to-face or web-based solutions.

'Just to let you know that of all the behavioural diagnostics, Myers Briggs's, personality inventories, capability checklists, psychology by numbers, etc. etc. which I've been subjected to over the last few years easily the most valuable and useful was the discussions we had and the report you produced for me. Your method has strong foundations and your analysis has depth which really resonated with me.' (Paul Lund)

'Andrew and I have known each other for seven years and he has excellent insight. He also has a very methodical process to help identify organisation talent through the RTPe process. His book and concept of the working journey is a must for any organisation in this difficult economic condition.' (RR Krishna, vice-president, FL Smidth, India)

- **Coaching and Mentorship**. We offer a range of customised programmes globally.

'Andrew has a wonderful insight into how people should run businesses and coaches to maximising the individuals' potential. A high level deep strategist and a wonderful person!' (Gareth Ackerman, Chairman, Pick n Pay, South Africa)

With Thanks

I am indebted to the knowledge and understanding passed on by my early mentors; particularly Robin Mills—my last and best 'boss', and Gillian Stamp—my one-time mentor. I am also indebted to Elliott Jaques, not only for his insights and research, but for pointing out to me that I was only at the start of the journey when I thought I had 'arrived'. I would also like to acknowledge Barry and Sheila Deane, who showed me how it could all be integrated into one body of accessible knowledge.

Also to my clients, some of whom have been great teachers. A special thanks to Ian Stone, Mike Hawker, my colleagues, and contributors to this book; Christoffer and Azuncena, all of whom generously offered contributions to this book. Thanks to Verena MacLean for her support and for sharing her work at MTN and to Adam Thompson for comments and contributions.

I hope this book serves to introduce many new Managerial Leaders to these essential principles of their profession.

Andrew Olivier

Notes and Bibliography

1 Major works include *The Changing Culture of a Factory* (1951), *Management of Responsibility* (1956), *Equitable Payment* (1961), *A General Theory of Bureaucracy* (1976), *The Form of Time* (1982), *Requisite Organisation* (1988), *Creativity and Work* (1990), *Requisite Organisation: A Total System for Effective Managerial Organisation and Managerial Leadership for the 21st Century* (1997).

Section I

2 Gray, J. L. (ed) (1976). *The Glacier Project: Concepts and Critiques: Selected Readings on the Glacier Theories of Organisation and Management*. London: Heinemann Educational Books.

3 Global Organisation Design Society (http://globalro.org) is a not-for-profit organisation, and it is included as a key contributor because it has drawn together many of the players, case studies, and legacy into one website. It has been active in building a community and in furthering knowledge of these approaches.

4 Brown, J. (2011). *The Legacy of Elliott Jaques*. International Journal of Applied Psychoanalytic Studies 8 (1), pp. 89-94. Published online 19 January 2011 in Wiley Online Library http://onlinelibrary.wiley.com/doi/10.1002/aps.273/abstract.

5 Boedker, Vidgen, Meagher, Cogin, Mouristen, Runnals (2011). Australian School of Business. Society of knowledge Economics. Viewed online at http://www.ske.org.au/download/SKE_2011_High_Performing_Workplaces_Index_October_6_2011_FINAL.pdf.

6 Allen. T. F. H. (2001). *Hierarchy Theory in Ecology*. Entry in the Encyclopedia of Environmetrics. New Jersey, NJ: Wiley.

7 GO Society Editorial Board (2010). *US Army use of Requisite Organisation since 1978*. Download case studies, interviews, publications at http://globalro.org/en/go-library/case-studies.html.

8 Zaccaro, Stephen J. (October 1996). *Models and Theories of Executive Leadership. A Conceptual/Empirical Review and Integration*. US Army Research Institute for the Behavioural and Social Sciences. See also Harris, Patricia, and Lucas, Kenneth W. (1994). *Executive Leadership: Requisite Skills and Developmental Processes for Three and Four-Star Assignments*, NTIS Springfield, VA, 22161. And Lucas, Kenneth W. and Joan Markessini (1993). *Senior Leadership in a Changing World Order: Requisite Skills for US Army One-and Two-Star Assignments*, NTIS, Springfield, VA, 22161.

9 Novus International (2010). *Requisite Organisation at Novus International. Management Brief White Paper to employees and stakeholders*. Download at Global RO. Org at http://globalro.org/en/2010-09-13-08-13-06/the-novus-international-story.html. See also at same location Lee, Nancy R, The Novus Story and International and Global RO and Lee, Nancy, R. (2009). *The Practice of Managerial Leadership. The Novus Story*, Chapter 6. p. 174. El Escribo. Buenos Aires.

10 Go Society Editorial Board (2010). *Application of Requisite Organisation Concepts in Mining and Heavy Manufacturing Organisations* (Glacier Metal Company, CRA/Rio Tinto, Acindar, Anglo Gold Ashanti, Algoma Steel, CONARCO, Tata Group etc.) Download case studies, interviews, publications at http://globalro.org/2010-09-13-08-13-06/mining-and-heavy-manufacturing.html#Acindar%20Steel.

11 Raven, P. *Sustainability in an Interconnected World*. Malcolm MacIntosh Memorial Lecture 2001. Canberra: CSIRO.

12 Jaques, Elliott. *Requisite Organisation*. Cason Hall, p. 35, 1989.

13 Adapted from various sources including: Lewis, P. (1989). *Transformational Change using Stratified Systems Theory*. International Journal of Public Administration. 19 (6), pp. 801-826. Acknowledgements to Jaques, E. *Requisite Organisation*. Cason Hall.

14 Adapted from Mant, A. *Intelligent Leadership*. p. 275 and Olivier, A. *A Practitioner's Guide to Level of Work Audits and Organisational Mapping*. 1996. rev. 1998, 2000. Third Foundation Systems. Unpublished manuscript. With acknowledgement to Bioss Southern Africa. Also see Olivier, A. *The Working Journey*. MacOlive Co., 2003.

15 Peet, David. See http://www.fdavidpeat.com/biography/biography.htm David Peet runs a range of interesting course from his learning centre, a medieval

Italian village in Tuscany called the Paris Centre. http://www.paricenter.com/.

16 Bohm, David. See http://www.david-bohm.net/.

17 Senge, Peter. (1990). *The Fifth Discipline*. Double Day/Currency.

18 Jaworski, Joe. (1998). *Synchronicity*. San Francisco, CA: BK Publishers.

19 Elliott Jaques, E. (1989). *Requisite Organisation*. Arlington, VA: Cason Hall & Company; Jaques, E. and Clement, S. D. *Executive Leadership: A Practical Guide to Managing Complexity*, Blackwell, Oxford, UK and Cason Hall, Gloucester, MA. (Comment: A solid introductory book.)

20 See for example, *Is Your Team Too Big? Too Small? What's the Right Number? Knowledge at Wharton. June 14, 2006*. Viewed at http://knowledge.wharton.upenn.edu/article.cfm?articleid=1501. Also *Setting your Optimal Team Size* with I Opt Technology—posted 7 Jan 2008. Viewed on http://www.youtube.com/watch?v=00zae1QgH5U.

21 Branson, Richard. (2008). *Business Stripped Bare*. London: Virgin Books.

22 Lovelock, James. (2006). *The Revenge of Gaia*. Penguin Allan Lane; Lovelock, James. (2000). *Homage to Gaia. The Life of an Independent Scientist*. Oxford University Press.

23 Gladwell, Malcolm. (2000). *The Tipping Point*. Abacus Books.

24 W. L Gore & Associates. See http://www.gore.com/en_xx/news/FORTUNE2009.html.

25 Ibid., p. 184.

26 Olivier, A. (2007). *The Working Journey of Muhammad Yunus*. (2007). Global Organisation Design. Downloadable at http://globalro.org/en/go-library/articles-excerpts-a-chapters/918-the-working-journey-of-muhammad-yunus.html. Also downloadable at http://www.theworkingjourney.com/165

27 Yunus, Muhammad. (2003). *Banker to the Poor*. Aurum Press. p. 142.

28 Gates, (2007). 'Too big for its boots—consumer fury and a raft of court cases over microsoft's trading practices—has Bill Gates's baby overreached itself.' *New Scientist*. no. 2111.

29 Semler, R. (1993). *Maverick*. New York, NY: Warner Books.

30 Acknowledgement to Adam Thompson, who raised this point in discussion with author and quoted with permission.

31 MacLean, V. *MTN: Case Study of Complexity in a Growth Strategy*. Paper presented at the Third Biennal Global Organisation Design Conference, Argentina: Buenos Aires. 2009.

32 Kirkpatrick, D. (2010). *The Facebook Effect: The Inside Story of the Company that is Connecting the World*. Simon & Schuster Paperback. p. 271.

33 From an Interview with the author on a large, complex, cross functional project. 2008. This project is used again to illustrate the consequences of failing to apply Principle 5.

34 Lashinksy, Adam. *How Apple Works: Inside The World's Largest Startup*. Fortune Magazine, 23 May 2011. Also viewed on CNN Money, 17 May 2012 at http://tech.fortune.cnn.com/2011/08/25/how-apple-works-inside-the-worlds-biggest-startup/

35 Lee, Nancy, R. (2009). *The Practice of Managerial Leadership*. El Escriba, Buenos Aires.

36 This case study is based on fact and the quotes are actual comments made. The identity of the organisation and individuals quoted remains confidential.

37 Rapid Talent Pool Evaluation is a process based on requisite practices pioneered by Elliott Jaques and is described in **Requisite Organisation**, Page Pair 112 and in Jaques, E. J. and Clement, S. (2002). *Executive Leadership. A Practical Guide to Managing Complexity*. Blackwell Publishing. p. 250.

Section II

38 Hoebeke, L. (1994). *Making Work Systems Better. A Practitioner's Reflections*. Wiley. *Note:* A later and significant contributor, Luc Hoebeke, added significantly to our understanding through the conceptualisation of 'domains of work' in which he grouped the levels of work called process levels. Hoebeke's understanding of process levels saw work systems as being systems of self-regulated, semi-autonomous networks, which are connected together in varying degrees of tight/loose properties. Each process level within a work system has unique outputs and are arranged in an work network. These works systems can quickly reconfigure and form new networks 1994. Also Olivier, A. *A Practitioners Guide to Level of Work Audits and Organisational Mapping*. 1996. revised 1998. Third Foundation Systems. Unpublished manuscript.

39 In compiling this Handbook I wanted to add a military case study, other than the US Army which is well documented. Jaques and colleagues did extensive work with the US military. His work with human capability and its mirror construct, Levels of Work (which he originally called Stratified Systems Theory) was comprehensively adopted and is still used by the US Army. It was introduced in a post-Vietnam restructure when a Four Star Command was created to manage organizational transformation. Extensive research was done on by the US Army Research Institute into the validity

of Jaques concepts and it published its findings in a series of papers over a decade.

It is reported that Generals Colin Powell and Norman Swarzkopff both went through capability interviews as discussed in Principle 6 (Match Capability to Role). In 1997 I presented a paper on Third Wave Warfare, human capability and Levels of Work and spoke to the South African National Defense Force (SANDF) Defense Parliamentary subcommittee on defence restructure. In 2000 I submitted a paper to an Australian Federal Government Review on capability of the ADF and in 2004 the ADF Joint Chiefs of Staff went through capability interviews, followed up in 2005 by an additional 40 mid-career officers undertaking similar capability interviews.

Alvin Toffler in his book 'War and Anti-War wrote with remarkable prescience about how the role of Special Forces would increase in importance as the world splintered and the case of Executive Outcomes validated his hypothesis. Having served briefly with Eeben Barlow made this story possible.

40 The Private Military Companies (PMC) is the evolutionary development of what is arguably the second oldest profession in the world. A PMC is a legally established enterprise that makes a profit and has corporate structures staffed by well-trained officers, NCOs, and men. PMCs may use armed force, hence defined as: *legally established enterprises that make a profit by either providing services involving the potential exercise of [armed] force in a systematic way and by military means, and/or by the transfer of that potential to clients through training and other practices, such as logistics support, equipment procurement, and intelligence gathering.* Conflict Incorporated: Selling the Art of War.

Transcript from *http://www.cdi.org/adm/1113/transcript.html* Produced December 7, 1997. Also see http://www.privatemilitary.org.

41 In 1981, I met Eeben Barlow, when I was an officer in the Marines, and he was Sapper officer. I recognised in him a spark that many years later I would be able to identify as high potential. He was also English speaking, like myself in a predominantly Afrikaans speaking military structure, where English speakers were also discriminated.

42 Hoebeke, L. (1994). *Making Work Systems Better.* Wiley. p. 63.

43 Stamp, G. *Managing Uncertainty and Complexity*. Third Foundations System Conference. BIOSS Johannesburg. June 1996.

44 Dive, Brian. (2002). *The Healthy Organisation*. Kogan Page.

45 Barclays CEO Diamond quits over rate rigging. Read online at http://www.brisbanetimes.com.au/business/world-business/barclays-ceo-diamond-quits-over-rate-rigging-20120704-21g1o.html

46 Brand, S. (1999). *The Clock of the Long Now. Time and Responsiblitiy*. Phoenix.

47 Collins, Jim. 'Level 5 Leadership. The Triumph of Humility and Fierce Resolve,' *Harvard Business Review*, Jan. 2001.

48 GlaxoSmithLine fined $3bn after bribing doctors to increase drug sales - read online at http://www.guardian.co.uk/business/2012/jul/03/glaxosmithkline-fined-bribing-doctors-pharmaceuticals?newsfeed=true

49 Charles Taylor and other guilty of war crimes were convicted by the Special Court for Sierra Leone in 2012, the first head of state to be prosecuted for crimes against humanity. See online at http://en.wikipedia.org/wiki/Special_Court_for_Sierra_Leone and The Trial of Charles Taylor at http://www.charlestaylortrial.org/trial-background/who-is-charles-taylor/

50 Virgin King. p. 78.

51 Olivier, A. Correspondence with Prof. Muhammad Yunus. 2007, 2009; and Prasso, Sheridan. 'Saving the World with a Cup of Yoghurt', *Fortune Magazine*, Jan/Feb. 2007. no. 2; The News Desk. *The Daily Star* Bangladesh. 24 February 2007; also Wikipedia: the Free Encyclopaedia: http://en.wikipedia.org/wiki/Grameen_Bank and http://en.wikipedia.org/wiki/Muhammad_Yunus#Childhood_and_family; Yunus, M. and Jolis, A. (1988). *Banker to the Poor: The Story of the Grameen Bank*. Arum Press. Reprint 2003.

52 Yunus, Muhammad. *Social Business Entrepreneurs Are the Solution*. Downloaded extract from http://www.grameen-info.org/bank/socialbusinessentrepreneurs.htm on 18 May 2007.

53 For a greater understanding of his capability and its impact on his Work Journey see Olivier, A. (2007). *The Growth of Capability of Muhammad Yunus*. Online at Global Organisation Design *http://globalro.org* or download at *http://www.theworkingjourney.com/165*.

54 Peter Wrighton. Retired CEO. Premier Group. Winner of Nelson Mandela's CEO of the Year Award. From a Career Path Appreciation interview with Andrew Olivier. 1996.

55 Tesco—reference online at http://www.thetimes100.co.uk/case-study--skillsand-behaviours--132-323-3.php and see Dive, Brian.,(2002). *Healthy Organisation*—Kogan Page, for information on this project.

56 Piore, A. and Theil, S. 'The Teflon Multinational', *Newsweek*, 12 March 2001.

57 Branson, Richard. *Business Stripped Bare*. Penguin Books. 2008. pp. 230, 228, 276, 279.

58 Lovelock, James (2000). *Homage to Gaia: The Life of an Independent Scientist*. Oxford University.

59 Hoebeke, L. (1994). *Making Work Systems Better. A Practitioner's Reflections*. Wiley, p. 99.

60 Brause, A. (2000). *An Investigation of Presidential Elections Using Jaques' Construct of Mental Complexity*. Unpublished Doctoral Dissertation, University of Texas, Austin.

61 For more information on this amazing group, go to http://theelders.org.

62 The Virgin Brand. Marketing Minds. Viewed at http://www.marketingminds.com.au/branding/virgin.html on May 29, 2010.

63 Acknowledgment and thanks. NASA, photos from http://www.nasa.gov/vision/earth/lookingatearth/NIGHTLIGHTS.html. Viewed on 1 July 2012.

64 DeCarlo, Scott. *Forbes*. Viewed online at http://www.forbes.com/sites/scottdecarlo/2012/04/18/the-worlds-biggest-companies/on 1 July 2012 and Wikipedia List of Companies by Revenue. Viewed online at http://en.wikipedia.org/wiki/List_of_companies_by_revenue on 1 July 2012.

65 Diamond, Jared (2005). *Collapse* Allan Lane, an imprint of Penguin Books.

66 Gilding, Paul.(2011). The *Great Disruption*. Bloomsbury Publishing Plc.

Section III

67 See the following two blogs by Michael Kromwyk—http://charmike4.hubpages.com/hub/RequisiteOrganisationandLevelsofWorkARealLifeExample and http://charmike4.hubpages.com/hub/Training-and-Development-Requisite-Organisation.

68 Mant, A. (1997). *Intelligent Leadership*. New South Wales: Allen Unwin. p. 277.

Index of Figures

	Title	Page
Figure 1	**Domains and levels of work**	29
Figure 2	**Mutual Knowledge Recognition units**	36
Figure 3	**SemCo org chart design with work levels**	39
Figure 4	**A level IV led business**	43
Figure 5	**A level V led business**	44
Figure 6	**A level VI led business**	46
Figure 7	**MTN organic growth**	48
Figure 8	**The levels of work model showing unique value add and time span**	53
Figure 9	**Example of a function review**	55
Figure 10	**The level of work of a role**	58
Figure 11	**What are we looking at structurally?**	60
Figure 12	**The MoR accountabilities**	74
Figure 13	**Passage of leadership**	75
Figure 14	**A matrix of working relationships**	81
Figure 15	**Process flow across Convention and Events Centre**	85
Figure 16	**Domains and levels of work (repeat of Figure 1)**	97
Figure 17	**Our species covers the globe**	184
Figure 18a	**Old Structure of Road Service**	208
Figure 18b	**New Structure of Road Service**	209

Figure 18c	**Old Structure of Roadside Assistance Centre**	210
Figure 18d	**New Structure of Roadside Assistance Centre**	211
Figure 19a	**Transition structure of Corporate Office**	227
Figure 19b	**Organisational structure of each country**	228

Index of Tables

	Title	Page
Table 1	**Levels of work complexity**	27
Table 2	**Characteristics of the structure templates**	49
Table 3	**Line management role authorities**	71
Table 4	**Specialist/non-managerial role authorities**	78

Index

A

accountability:
  broad areas of 73f
  for effectiveness and performance 67
  of managers 71, 114
  meaning of 64
  organisational perspective of 68
AMG Consulting 218
Andersson, Christoffer 191
authority 61, 63, 69, 207
  broad areas of 73f
  for effectiveness and performance 67
  line-management role of 71f
  managerial 65, 69
  meaning of 64
  minimum managerial *see* VARI

B

Barlow, Eeben 25, 152 *see also* Executive Outcomes
BHP Billiton 12, 175
Bohm, David 30
Branson, Richard 25, 35 *see also* Virgin
Brown, Wilfred 10
Buffet, Warren 161
business intent *see* Principle 1

C

CAC (current actual capability) 86, 88
Capital Allocation 161
CAS (complex adaptive system) 21-2, 151
case studies 79-81, 105
  by AMG Consulting 218-32
  on Executive Outcomes 116, 123, 125, 134, 138, 148
  on Grameen Bank 153-8, 173, 183
  on RAA 198-216
  on Tesco 166-7
  on Virgin 125-53, 173, 178-82
Collapse (Diamond) 187
Collins, Jim 146
complexity 21
complexity science 21, 233
compliance 53, 55, 160-1, 188
CP (Cognitive Power) 86-8, 170, 180
creativity 36, 99, 104, 107-8, 113, 119, 123, 130, 143, 154, 164, 239

in work level I 107
in work level II 113
in work level III 119
in work level IV 130-2
in work level V 143-4
in work level VI 164

D

decision-making 104
consequence of 164
time span of 10, 92, 185
time to impact of 54, 104, 163-4
in work level I 107
in work level II 113
in work level III 119
in work level IV 129
in work level V 141
in work level VI 163
in work level VII 176
decision-taking 26
design 34, 54
Diamond, Jared 187

E

Elders 180-1
EQ *see* Wi (wisdom)
equilibrium 21
Ericsson India 196

F

Facebook 23, 52, 87, 145, 241
Findhorn 40
fractal patterns 167

G

Gates, Bill 37, 138, 179, 182
Gilding, Paul 187
Gisborne, Craig 40
Glacier Project 10
Gladwell, Malcolm 35
global competition 163
Global Organisation Design Conference 13, 241
Global Organisation Design Society 11-13, 239
Google 145, 192
Graicunas, A. V. 33
Grameen Bank 153-8, 173-4, 183
Great Disruption, The (Gilding) 187

H

Hoebeke, Luc 28, 180, 242-3, 245
human capability 12, 87

J

Jaques, Elliott 9-13
on business intent 140, 142
on decision-making 113
on human capability 87
on minimum managerial authority 69
RO model of 31, 224
on time span 52, 177
on work level VII 186

K

K/S/E (knowledge/skills/experience) 87-8
KRA (key results area) 56

L

leader(s):
managerial 57, 66, 68, 71, 90
project 72
role of 185
team 32
leadership 10-12, 25, 74-5, 99, 101-2, 105, 109, 114-15, 122, 133, 145-6, 160-1, 165, 177-8, 231-2
ensuring coherence in *see* Principle 7
passage of 75
science-based *see* RO (requisite organisation)
in work level I 109
in work level II 115, 117, 205
in work level III 122
in work level IV 133
in work level V 145-6
in work level VI 165
in work level VII 178
in work level VIII 187
Lee, Nancy R. 78
'Legacy of Elliott Jaques, The' (Brown) 11, 239
'Level 5 Leadership' (Collins) 146, 244
Lovelock, James 35, 152, 171

M

managers 71, 89-90
Mant, Alistair 233
MKU (Mutual Knowledge Unit) 33, 36f
Monger, Charlie 161
MoR (manager once removed) 34, 45, 90
accountability and authority of 74
becoming operative 120
review 203, 205
MRU (Mutual Recognition Unit) 40
MTN (Mobile Telephone Networks) 47

O

optimal size *see* Principle 2
organisational structure 31, 45, 65, 104, 108, 114, 120, 132, 144, 165, 177, 193, 228, 232
distance in vertical *see* Principle 4
principles of 92 *see also* individual principles
of work level I 108
of work level II 114
of work level III 122
of work level IV 133
of work level V 145
of work level VI 165
of work level VII 177
organisations 31, 41

P

PD (position descriptions) 51, 53, 55-7, 90
Peat, David 31
performance 22-3, 63-4, 66-7, 69, 77, 87, 105, 109-10, 115, 118, 122-3, 134, 142, 146-7, 165-7
ensuring 63
issues in 77
in work level I 109
in work level II 116
in work level III 123
in work level IV 134, 142

in work level V 147
in work level VI 166
in work level VII 175
performance management 203-5
PM (project manager) 72
PMC (private military company) 116
Popper, Karl 11
Powell, Colin 12, 243
Practice of Managerial Leadership, The (Lee) 78, 240, 242
Prigogine, Illya 21
Principle 1 *20-30, 51*
Principle 2 *30-42, 51, 92*
Principle 3 59, *92, 236*
applied in level V 140
as a key accountability 129
Principle 4 *32, 59-63, 93*
in work level III 120
Principle 5 *58, 63-85, 91-93*
Principle 6 89, *93, 141, 182*
Principle 7 *89-93, 146*

R

RAA (Royal Automobile Association of South Australia) 121, 198, 200-1, 207, 214
reporting distance *see* Principle 4
requisite, law of 20, 23
resource management 165
resources 23, 26-7, 63-4, 77-8, 97-100, 105, 108-9, 111-12, 115, 117-18, 122, 128-9, 131-2, 134, 165-6
in work level I 109
in work level II 115
in work level III 122
in work level IV 134
in work level V 146
in work level VI 165
responsibility:
commitment to 195
meaning of 64
of MoR 73
social 100, 165
RO (requisite organisation) 13
structure of 224
role complexity 33, 47 *see also* Principle 6
role design 13
role relationships 63, 90
empowering *see* Principle 5
specialists 76
task assigning *see* TARR (task assigning role relationship)
task initiating *see* TIRR (task initiating role relationship)
role(s) 63
cross-functional 69, 81, 84 *see also* TIRR (task initiating role relationship)
line-management 65, 68-9
authorities of 71f
subsets of 74
nonmanagerial 78t, 82
RTPe (rapid talent pool evalutaion) 87, 202

S

scenario planning 163
Semco 37, 39f
Semler, Ricardo 37, 241
Senge, Peter 30
sequence of events 19, 50, 57, 63, 197
service-providing function 77
span of control 33-4
Stamp, Gillian 9, 130, 142, 243
stasis *see* equilibrium

Stone, Ian 198, 202
strategic differentiation 161
Successful Habits of Visionary Companies (Collins) 146
supervisor 72
Sustainability 101, 147, 165, 224
sustainability, corporate 28t, 185, 187
Synchronicity (Jaworski) 30

T

T (temperament) 88, 239
talent pool 35, 73-4, 193, 202
TARR (task assigning role relationship) 68, 76, 205
Tesco 166-7
time span 52-5, 104
  for work level I 107
  for work level II 113
  for work level III 119
  for work level IV 130
  for work level V 143
  for work level VI 163-4
  for work level VII 176
Tipping Point 35, 241
Tipping Point (Gladwell) 35
TIRR (task initiating role relationship) 76, 205
  across the organization 85
  establishing authorities for 81-3

U

US Army 12
UVA (unique value add) 20, 22, 26-7, 37, 52-4, 56, 59-63, 65, 71, 73, 89-90, 140-1, 150-1, 181, 205-6

V

V (values) 88
VARI 69-72, 74
Virgin 25, 87, 105, 125, 138-9, 145, 150, 152-3, 170-3, 178
Virgin Galactic 171, 178-80
vulnerabilities 99-100, 104, 107, 113-14, 119, 130-1, 143, 153, 163-4, 169, 202, 205
  of work level I 107
  of work level II 114
  of work level III 119
  of work level IV 132
  of work level V 143-4
  of work level VI 164

W

Wi (wisdom) 88
WL Gore and Associates 35
work 41, 84, 98 *see also* Principle 3
  system of 51
  undefined 57
work complexity 22, 27t, 95 *see also* Principle 1
work domain(s) 29, 97f
  added value 75, 97
  innovative 99-100
  values 75, 101-3
work level(s) 22, 24, 26t, 28-9
  I (quality) 23, 109-10
  II (service) 52, 71, 111-17, 168-9
  III (practice) 52, 82, 85, 98, 121-2, 125-6
  IV (strategic development) 42, 43f, 53, 130-2, 135-9, 168
  V (strategic intent) 43-4, 44f, 142-3, 145, 147, 149, 151-2, 157-8

VI (corporate citizenship) 44-174
VII (corporate prescience) 46, 178, 180, 182-3, 186
VIII (corporate sustainability) 188
analysis of 37
role 58-9
structure descriptions of 104

Y

Yunus, Muhammad 25, 153, 171, 179 *see also* Grameen Bank

Z

Zuckerberg, Mark 23, 26, 52, 152

20661274R00154

Printed in Great Britain
by Amazon